Collins | English for Exam

Cambridge English Qualifications

Activities for
B1 Preliminary
for Schools

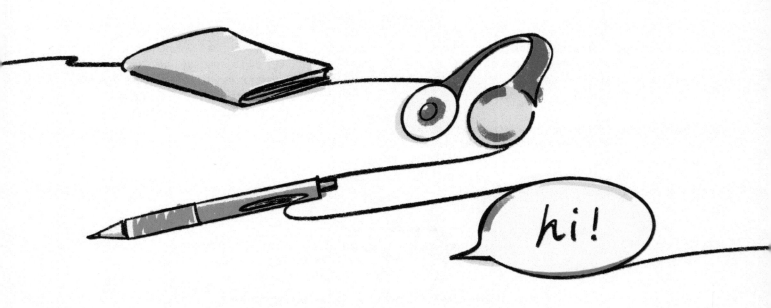

Published by Collins
An imprint of HarperCollins Publishers
Westerhill Road
Bishopbriggs
Glasgow
G64 2QT

HarperCollins Publishers, 1st Floor,
Watermarque Building, Ringsend Road,
Dublin 4, Ireland

First edition 2021

10 9 8 7 6 5 4 3 2 1

© HarperCollins Publishers 2021

ISBN 978-0-00-846117-1

Collins® is a registered trademark of
HarperCollins Publishers Limited

www.collins.co.uk/elt

A catalogue record for this book is available from
the British Library.

HarperCollins does not warrant that any website
mentioned in this title will be provided uninterrupted,
that any website will be error-free, that defects will be
corrected, or that the website or the server that makes
it available are free of viruses or bugs. For full terms
and conditions please refer to the site terms provided
on the website. If you would like to comment on any
aspect of this book, please contact us at the given
address or online.
E-mail: dictionaries@harpercollins.co.uk
 facebook.com/collinselt
@CollinsELT

Author: Rebecca Adlard
Series editor: Celia Wigley
For the Publisher: Gillian Bowman and Kerry Ferguson
Typesetter: Davidson Publishing Solutions
Artwork: Aptara (pages 17, 33, 53 and 59) and
Q2A Media (pages 31, 33, 55 and 73)
Audio: Tracks 9, 20, 34 and 44 recorded by Dsound.
All other audio recorded and produced by Tom Ottway,
Language Umbrella Media
Cover illustration © Maria Herbert-Liew 2021
All images from Shutterstock
Printed and Bound in the UK using 100% Renewable
Electricity at CPI Group (UK) Ltd

About the author
Rebecca Adlard is an experienced ELT professional
specialising in very young and young learners. She has
over 20 years' ELT experience and has taught English
and worked on various language projects in the UK,
Sweden, Denmark, Australia, Syria, China and Spain.
She is co-director of Language Umbrella Ltd.

MIX
Paper from
responsible sources
FSC™ C007454

FSC
www.fsc.org

This book is produced from independently certified FSC™ paper
to ensure responsible forest management.

For more information visit: www.harpercollins.co.uk/green

Dear Student

Welcome to Collins Activities for B1 Preliminary for Schools!

Here's some information on how to use this book so that you get the most out of your studies.

This book has 20 units and each unit covers a different topic. The topics and vocabulary in this book are from the official 2020 Cambridge B1 Preliminary for Schools Vocabulary List. This means that the words you are learning will help you do well in the Cambridge B1 Preliminary for Schools exam. I suggest you do the units in the order they appear as they get a little bit more difficult as you go along.

Each unit has activities that practise the four skills that are in the test: reading, writing, listening and speaking. There are also fun activities practising vocabulary, spelling and grammar.

The reading, writing, listening and speaking activities are similar to those in the exam. Next to each activity, you'll see a note to say which part of the official Cambridge B1 Preliminary for Schools test the activity is practising. For example, if you are doing a Reading activity and you see **PART 1**, this means the activity is preparation for Reading Part 1 of the test.

There is audio for the listening and speaking activities, which will also help your pronunciation. If you see this icon 🎧, please listen to the audio, which you can find online at www.collins.co.uk/eltresources. The track number is under the icon. In the listening part of the exam, the audio is played twice. So I suggest you play the audio for the listening activities twice.

If you see this icon ✌, this is a helping hand. It means that the information here can help you improve your English or help you do better in the exam.

At the front of the book, you will find the Contents table showing you what's in every unit. At the back of the book, you will find the answers, the audio scripts and the word lists for each unit.

I hope you enjoy using this book. Good luck with your studies!

Rebecca Adlard

(the author)

contents

Vocabulary

1 Listen and write each word under the correct photo.

1

_____

2

_____

3

_____

4

_____

5

_____

6

_____

7

_____

8

_____

9

_____

10

_____

11

_____

12
_____

2 Match the words with their definitions.

> kit   label   laundry   make-up   material
> pattern   pocket   size   underwear   uniform

1 _____: clothes and other things that are going to be washed

2 _____: the part of a piece of clothing that you can put things in

3 _____: the special clothes that some people wear to work or school

4 _____: a piece of paper or plastic attached to an object to give information about it

5 _____: clothes that you wear next to your skin, under your other clothes

6 _____: what clothes are made out of

7 _____: the creams and powders a person puts on their face to make them look attractive

8 _____: the set of clothes needed to play a particular sport

9 _____: how big or small something is

10 _____: an arrangement of lines or shapes that form a design

3 Choose the correct adjective from the box to complete each sentence.

cotton   plastic   silk   woollen

1 Nina is wearing a yellow _____ jumper and hat.

2 Jack is wearing a white _____ T-shirt.

3 Lena is wearing a colourful _____ scarf.

4 Ralph is wearing a yellow _____ raincoat.

Grammar: Present continuous: to talk about what is happening now

Ralph's *wearing* a yellow raincoat. He's *not wearing* a blue scarf.

Answer the questions. Write full sentences.
1 What are you wearing? What aren't you wearing?
2 What are you doing now?
3 What are your parents doing now?

Speaking

PART 1

Listen and answer the questions about clothes and accessories.

1 Tell me about the clothes you like.

2 How often do you buy new clothes? Where do you buy them from?

3 Do you wear a uniform to school?

4 Do you like to wear the same clothes as your friends? Why or why not?

5 What jewellery do you wear most days? What accessories do you carry most days?

Speaking tip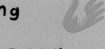

In Speaking Part 1, if you don't understand what the examiner says, you should ask them to repeat it. Use these phrases:

Sorry, can you repeat that, please?

Could you say that again, please?

Reading

Read the text about a social app called *Dress-up*.

Five sentences have been removed from the text.

For each question, choose the correct answer.

There are three extra sentences which you do not need to use.

Dress-up
By Hannah, aged 13

I wanted to buy my dad an expensive present for his birthday, but I didn't have any money. **(1)** _____ But they only earn about £4 each time and I needed a lot of money.

I didn't know what to do until my mum came in to my bedroom with some clean clothes. **(2)** _____ She said that I had too many clothes and that I should take out the ones I didn't wear.

So, I made a pile of the clothes that were too small for me or that I didn't really like anymore. And then I thought maybe instead of giving them away I could sell them. I found a social app called Dress-up online. People use the app to buy other people's old clothes. All you have to do is to take photos of the clothes you don't want and upload them to the app. **(3)** _____ If someone buys something from you, you post it to them. The app takes 10% of the money you make.

I put all the clothes I didn't want on the app. Not all of them were bought, but lots were. **(4)** _____ I couldn't have made that much money from walking people's dogs or doing a neighbour's shopping. **(5)** _____ And the best thing is my dad got a really lovely birthday present and that made him very happy.

A Now all my friends want to do the same thing.

B I made £80 in four weeks.

C I bought lots of things, including some great jeans.

D Some of my friends walk people's dogs or do their neighbour's shopping for them.

E Another idea is to take your old clothes to a charity shop.

F I told her there was no space in my wardrobe to put them.

G You also have to decide a price for each thing.

H My mum offered to lend me the money, but I said no.

8

Listening

For each question, write the correct answer in the gap. Write *one* or *two words*, or a *number*, or a *date*, or a *time*.

You will hear a woman called Kitty Hall telling a group of students about her work as a fashion designer.

Fashion designer

Kitty started to work at the clothes shop full time at the age of (1) _____.

She went to college when she was (2) _____.

In her first job after college, she designed (3) _____.

Kitty's favourite thing to design is (4) _____.

Listening tip

In Listening Part 3, read the sentences carefully before you listen. They are a summary of the content you will hear. Think about what the missing information is likely to be. For example, Kitty left school *at the age of…* is likely to be a number.

Writing

Write your answer in about 100 words.

You see this announcement on the school noticeboard.

NEW SCHOOL UNIFORM

As you know, we are changing the school uniform for all students next year. We would like to know what students think the new school uniform should be like. Please send an email to your teacher, describing what new school uniform you would like to have. Please consider both boys' and girls' uniforms. You can also tell us what jewellery or accessories you think students should be allowed to wear at school.

writing tip

You could use these phrases in this writing task:
I think that…
In my opinion, …
I would/wouldn't like to have/wear…
… should be allowed…
(to wear)

Write an email to your teacher.

Grammar: Present continuous: to talk about future plans

We *are changing* the school uniform *next year*. (= we have already agreed this/ there are already plans for this) Answer the question. Write a full sentence.

What are you doing next weekend?

Vocabulary

🎧 **1 Listen and tick the correct photo.**

4

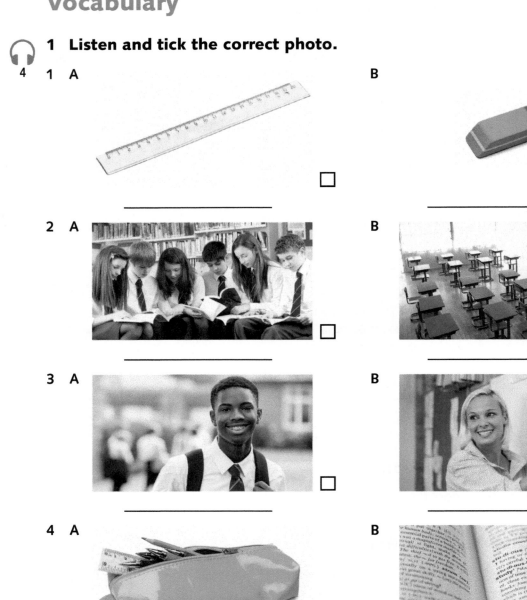

1 A   B

☐   ☐

_____ _____

2 A   B

☐   ☐

_____ _____

3 A   B

☐   ☐

_____ _____

4 A   B

☐   ☐

_____ _____

5 A   B

☐   ☐

_____ _____

🎧 **2 Write the words under the photos in Exercise 1. Then listen and check.**

5

3 Choose the correct words to complete the texts.

My grandad left school when he was 14. He didn't take any **(1)** *research / exams* so he hasn't got any **(2)** *qualifications / marks*. But my grandma went to **(3)** *university / primary school*, and she has a **(4)** *degree / test* in economics.

In nature studies, we are doing a **(5)** *project / subject* on wild flowers that grow in the region where we live. This weekend we have to do lots of **(6)** *registers / research*. Our teacher wants us to go for a walk and take photos of all the wild flowers we see. Then we have to find them on the internet and make **(7)** *notes / studies* about each one to bring to class next week.

My dad was very upset yesterday. He used to live in Japan, so he speaks Japanese, but he doesn't speak Japanese very often, so he doesn't **(8)** *remember / learn* some words and phrases. He decided to do a **(9)** *school / course* at the local **(10)** *classroom / college*. He thought he'd be advanced level, but when he took the Japanese test, he didn't get many marks, so the teacher told him he was only intermediate **(11)** *level / diploma*. Poor Dad!

My little sister, Eve, is only eight years old so she goes to **(12)** *primary / secondary* school. She doesn't like it very much. She's very **(13)** *absent / clever* but she chats a lot in class and never listens to the teacher, so she never understands what she should be doing in her **(14)** *lessons / instructions*.

Speaking

6

PART 2

Here is a photograph. It shows some children at school.
Tell me what you can see in the photograph.

Speaking tip

In Speaking Part 2, talk about:

• the people or person in the photograph

• the place in the photograph

• other things in the photograph.

Start with: *In this photo there is/are...*

**For each question, write the correct letter (A–F) next to each number.
There are two options you do not need to use.**

The young people below need to choose which art option to do at school this term.
Below there are descriptions of the six possible art options.
Decide which course (A–E) would be the most suitable for each person (1–4).

1  _____

Zoe loves art lessons. She'd like to be an artist when she is older and plans to do art at university. She'd like to try lots of different art techniques.

2  _____

Mike loves sports, but he's not that keen on art. However, he does quite like taking photos on his phone.

3  _____

Ellie is good at art. She likes experimenting with different techniques. She has done a painting and drawing course before and would like to try something different. She thinks it would be fun to make some clothes for herself and her sister.

4  _____

Dan likes art, but he prefers computers. His favourite subject at school is IT and he's keen to get a job in IT when he's older.

Art options this term

A Art option 1
Come and explore the world of photography. In this fun course you will use your phone and our digital cameras to learn how to take great photos and how to edit them. Students' photos will appear in an exhibition at the end of the term.

B Art option 2
You don't have to pick up a paintbrush to do amazing art! Come and explore digital art. All the art you will do in this course will be on a computer.

C Art option 3
If you love art, you'll love this course. Suitable for students with some experience and who are keen to progress and happy to work hard. The course focuses on improving painting and drawing skills.

D Art option 4
This course uses materials such as cotton, wool, plastic, leather and silk, and techniques such as sewing and knitting, to produce pieces of art. You will learn new skills and be encouraged to create a variety of clothing and accessories to take home.

E Art option 5
If you take this course, you'll learn a variety of art techniques, including painting, drawing, photography and sculpture. It's a great course for anyone who wants to explore all areas of art and to find out which form of art they like best.

F Art option 6
In this course you will design and create various objects from clay. You'll start with a teacup and saucer that you will be allowed to take home. Great idea for a Mother's Day present!

> **Grammar:** **First conditional: to talk about future situations we believe are real or possible**
>
> *If* you *take* this course, you*'ll learn* a variety of art techniques.
> Answer the questions. Write full sentences.
> **1** What will you do if it rains tomorrow?
> **2** What will you say if your mum or dad asks you to tidy your room?
> Remember: the negative of *will* is *won't*.

Listening

For each question, choose the correct answer.

7

1 **You will hear two friends talking about homework.**

The girl says that writing essays on a computer
A is slower than writing by hand.
B is quicker than writing by hand.
C helps you make fewer mistakes.

2 **You will hear a girl talking to her mum about college.**

The girl would like to study
A French, Spanish and art.
B Spanish, art and geography.
C Spanish, art and history.

Writing

Read this email from your English teacher, Ms Finch, and the notes you have made.

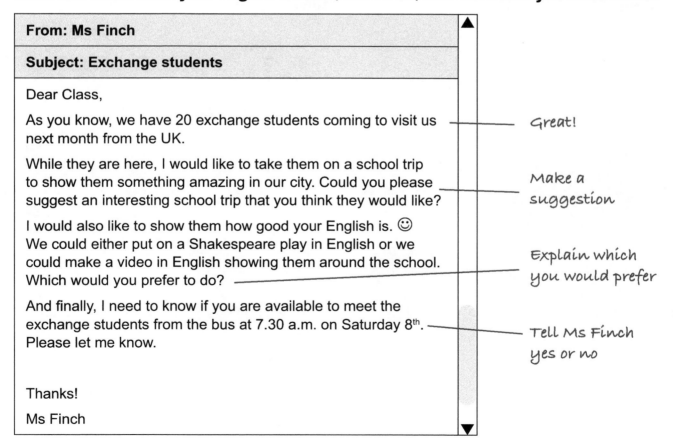

From: Ms Finch

Subject: Exchange students

Dear Class,

As you know, we have 20 exchange students coming to visit us next month from the UK. —— *Great!*

While they are here, I would like to take them on a school trip to show them something amazing in our city. Could you please suggest an interesting school trip that you think they would like? —— *Make a suggestion*

I would also like to show them how good your English is. ☺ We could either put on a Shakespeare play in English or we could make a video in English showing them around the school. Which would you prefer to do? —— *Explain which you would prefer*

And finally, I need to know if you are available to meet the exchange students from the bus at 7.30 a.m. on Saturday 8th. Please let me know. —— *Tell Ms Finch yes or no*

Thanks!

Ms Finch

Write your email to Ms Finch using all the notes.

Write about 100 words.

Vocabulary

1 Complete the crossword.

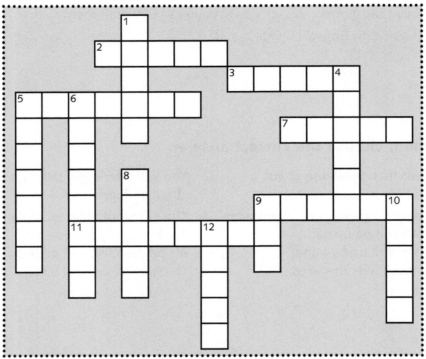

Across

2
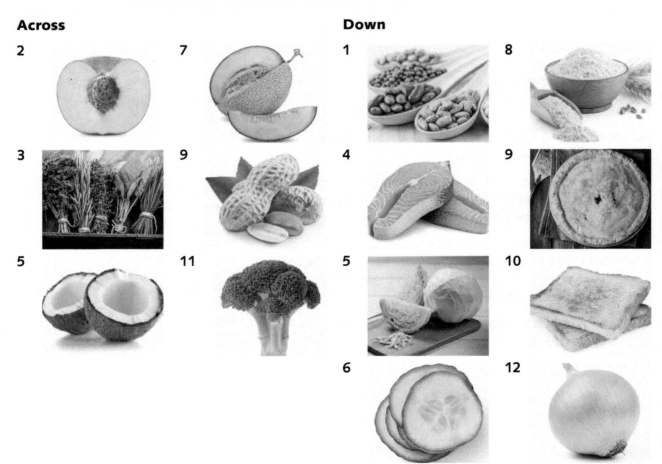

7

3

9

5

11

Down

1

8

4

9

5

10

6

12

2 Choose the correct word from the box to complete each sentence.

> ingredients   microwave   pan   recipe   refreshment
> slice   snack   sour   spicy   sweet   taste   vegetarian

1 'Janet, would you like a _____ of cake with your cup of tea?'

2 I'm going shopping to buy the _____ for tonight's dinner. I'm making a curry.

3 Jon always has a _____ when he gets home from school.

4 We use our tongue to _____ our food.

5 Lemons taste _____.

6 My friend David doesn't eat meat – he's _____.

7 If you want to cook some food very quickly, you can put it in the _____.

8 Patty loves _____ food, so I'm cooking fish with chillies for her.

9 Chocolate and cake have lots of sugar, so they taste _____.

10 'Will there be any _____ at the school play, or shall we take some sweets and a bottle of water with us?'

11 I always use my grandad's _____ when I make a birthday cake. It's the best and it never goes wrong!

12 'Shall I help you fry the sausages, Mum?'
'Yes, please! Can you put them in the _____? It's ready.'

Speaking

PART 3

Some students are having an end-of-term meal together. Here are some meals they are having. Describe each of the meals and say which would be most fun.

1

2

3

4

Speaking tip

In Speaking Part 3, you must discuss your opinions. Use phrases such as, *I think that...*; *In my opinion, ...*; *I suppose...*; *but I prefer...*

Try to give reasons to support your opinions using *because*.

15

Reading

Read the text about making a cottage pie.

For each question, choose the correct answer.

Cottage pie

Cottage pie is a traditional British meal. It's made from meat, vegetables and potatoes. To make a cottage pie you will need meat, onions, garlic, carrots, potatoes, herbs, butter, milk and tomatoes. First, **(1)** _____ the potatoes. Then use a **(2)** _____ knife to cut them. Fill a large **(3)** _____ with water. Add some salt. Put the potatoes in the water. Then boil them until they are soft.

While the potatoes are boiling, prepare the meat. **(4)** _____ an onion and some carrots into small pieces and fry them in a frying pan. Next, add some garlic and some herbs. Then add the meat and cook until it turns brown. Add some water and some tomatoes.

After that, take the potatoes out of the water. **(5)** _____ some butter and milk and mix with the potatoes.

Put the meat and vegetables in a dish. Place the cooked potato on top. Finally, if you like cheese, you can put some on the top of the pie. Then **(6)** _____ it in the oven for about 30 minutes.

It's delicious with cabbage!

1	**A** peel	**B** break	**C** tear	**D** open
2	**A** sweet	**B** sharp	**C** tasty	**D** bitter
3	**A** oven	**B** cup	**C** bowl	**D** saucepan
4	**A** Make	**B** Cut	**C** Put	**D** Do
5	**A** Add	**B** Remove	**C** Stir	**D** Make
6	**A** bake	**B** fry	**C** make	**D** boil

Grammar: **Adverbs of sequence: *first, next, then, after that, finally***
Use to describe the order in which two or more actions happen.

Next, add some garlic and some herbs. *Then* add the meat and cook until it turns brown. *After that*, take the potatoes out of the water.

Write a paragraph describing how to make a simple meal, for example, your favourite sandwich or salad. Use adverbs of sequence.

Listening

For each question, choose the correct answer.

9

1 What did the boy buy from the supermarket?

A ☐   B ☐   C ☐

2 What is the man going to have for lunch?

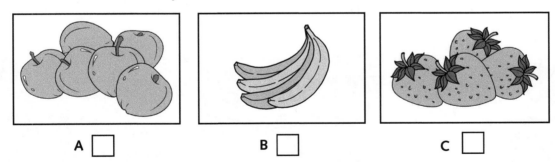

A ☐   B ☐   C ☐

3 Which fruit mustn't the boy eat?

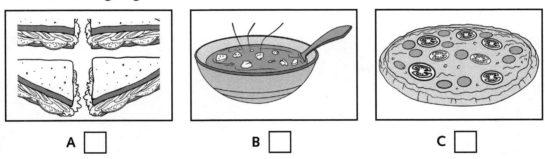

A ☐   B ☐   C ☐

Writing

Your English teacher has asked you to write a story.

Your story must begin with this sentence.

I wanted this to be the best meal Sarah had ever eaten.

Write your story in about 100 words.

Writing tip

In Writing Part 3, use adverbs of sequence in your writing to describe the order in which the main person or people in your story does things.

Vocabulary

1 Complete the words.

1 su _ ba _ _ _ _ g

2 playing g _ _ t _ _

3 _ _ k _ _ g

4 _ _ _ _ _ _ ting

5 playing _ _ _ _ _

6 at a f _ _ _ iv _ _

7 at a _ _ ll _ _ _

8 on a cr _ _ _ e

9 si _ _ tse _ _ _ _

10 sc _ _ _ t _ _ _

11 _ _ gg _ _ _

12 at a _ ar _ _

**2 Match a word from box A with a word from box B to make verbs.
Use the verbs in the correct form to complete the sentences below.**

A

go   hang   join   keen

B

in   on   out   shopping

1   It has finally stopped raining! We're _____ now.

2   I always _____ with my friends after school for an hour. Then I go home.

3   I like the countryside but I'm not very _____ camping.

4   Mum and I _____ yesterday because I needed a new school bag.

5   Ben isn't _____ with any of the games at the party. He's just playing on his phone!

**3 Match a word from box A with a word from box B to make compound nouns
to complete the sentences below.**

A

camp   ice   opening   play   sight

B

ground   hours   seeing   site   skates

1   The _____ was amazing – it had lots of space, a swimming pool and a playground.

2   I'm jealous – Sophie's got new _____. They're pale blue and she can go really fast with them.

3   We did lots of _____ in London. We saw Buckingham Palace, the Tower of London,
St Paul's Cathedral and the Houses of Parliament – all in one day!

4   The _____ for the school canteen are 7.00 to 8.30 a.m. and 12.00 midday to 1.30 p.m.

5   My younger brother wants me to take him to the _____ after school because there's a
new slide.

Speaking

PART 4

Listen and answer the questions about hobbies and leisure.

10

1   What do you like to do in your free time?

2   What do you think are the best hobbies or leisure activities
for children your age?

3   Tell me about a hobby you'd like to do. Think of something
you have never done.

4   Where do you like to hang out with your friends? Why?

5   What do you think the advantages and disadvantages are of
being a member of a club?

Reading

Read the text about Konrad. For each question, choose the correct answer.

A chess grandmaster

My name is Konrad. I'm 11 years old. I'm from Poland and I want to become a chess grandmaster. Chess grandmaster is the title given to the very best chess players in the world.

It all started when my family and I went to stay with my grandad one winter holiday. I wasn't very well, and I had to stay inside, so my grandad taught me to play chess. I was only five years old. I loved it! He told me about Sergei Karjakin who had also started playing chess when he was five – he became the youngest grandmaster ever at the age of 12. I decided that I wanted to be like Sergei.

My parents soon realised that I had a natural ability for the game. I told them again and again I wanted to be a professional. I was so keen on chess that I often played with my dad for three hours a day after school and then went to chess club as well! Other children were keen on sports like football, but this wasn't true for me.

I've already taken part in lots of chess competitions and I've won some of them. But what I really want is to be a grandmaster, like Sergei Karjakin. So, in March, I challenged the world chess champion, Luca Hoffman, to a match. I thought I was ready, even though Luca was 4 years older than me. I felt very calm and I played carefully, always defending instead of attacking. It was a long and difficult match. I got very tired. There was a point in the game when I thought I was going to win! But Luca is an excellent player and in the end I lost.

I won't let my defeat against Luca stop me. I've studied a lot since that match and I'm much better now. But I've decided that, to improve my chess skills further, I need to study with the best coach in the world in America. Although I'm only 11, my parents understand why I want to go and live abroad. They say I must wait until I'm 13, and then if I still want to go, they will help me. I think they understand that this is my dream.

1 What did Konrad's parents realise about him when he was about five years old?
   A that he had to choose between chess and other sports
   B that he was the youngest ever chess grandmaster
   C that he wanted to play chess with his father
   D that he was very good at and also keen on chess

2 During the match against Luca Hoffman, Konrad
   A was tired at first.
   B tried different ways to win.
   C nearly won the game.
   D nearly lost the game.

3 What might a journalist write about Konrad?
   A Konrad has a lot of talent and is lucky to have the support of his parents.
   B Konrad has not improved since his defeat against Luca Hoffman.
   C Konrad needs to improve his attitude to the game to be a top chess player.
   D Konrad could be a great player, but he needs to be more confident.

> **Reading tip**
>
> In Reading Part 3, the text is quite long. Skim it first to find out the topic, who the writer is and the general meaning. Then read it again, much more carefully, in order to understand the details and answer the questions.

Listening

11

For each question, write the correct answer in the gap. Write *one* or *two words*, or a *number*, or a *date*, or a *time*.

You will hear a woman called Lucy Jonson talking about her favourite hobby.

My favourite hobby

Lucy lives in the **(1)** _____ .

Her favourite hobby is **(2)** _____ .

She often writes for **(3)** _____ hours.

Lucy has written a book called **(4)** _____ .

She's not very good at **(5)** _____ .

Grammar: Second conditional: to imagine present or future situations that are impossible or unlikely to happen

If I *lived* in the city, I *would go* out with my friends to restaurants.

Answer the questions. Write full sentences.
1   What would you do if you met someone famous?
2   What would you do if you found a puppy in the street?

Remember: the negative of *would* is *wouldn't*.

Writing

Read this email from your ice-skating coach, Mr Hammond, and the notes you have made.

From: Mr Hammond
Subject: Ice-skating lessons this term
Dear club member, There will be three ice-skating club sessions on Mondays this term. — *Thanks for letting me know* The first session at 5.00 will be dancing on ice, the second at 5.45 will be ice-skating technique and the third at 6.30 will be advanced ice skating. Please let me know which session you would like to come to. — *Tell Mr Hammond choice and explain why* I also need to know if any club members would like to take an ice-skating exam this year or not. Let me know if you have any questions about these. — *Say yes; ask a question* I would also like to encourage more people to join the club. Please could all club members think of possible ways to find new members and let me know. — *Make a suggestion* See you all on Monday! Mr Hammond

Write your email to Mr Hammond using all the notes.

Write about 100 words.

Vocabulary

12

1 Listen and write the words in the correct places.

1 _____ 2 _____ 3 _____

4 _____

5 _____

6 _____

7 _____

10 _____ 9 _____ 8 _____

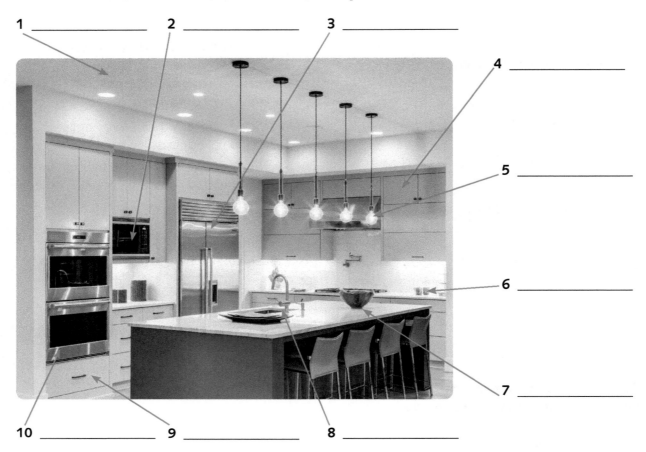

2 Match the words with their definitions.

| antique | blind | cellar | flatmate | handle | lock | neighbour | rent |

1 _____: a room underneath a building

2 _____: an old object that is valuable because of its beauty or the way it was made

3 _____: the part of a drawer or door that you pull to open it

4 _____: the part of a door or drawer you put a key in to open and close it

5 _____: a piece of cloth or other material that you can pull down over a window to cover it

6 _____: the money you pay a person who owns the house you live in

7 _____: someone who lives near or next to you

8 _____: a person who lives in the same house as you but is not a member of your family

3 Look at the photos. Match each sentence to a photo A, B, C or D.

A

B

C

D

		A	B	C	D
1	This is a cottage.	A	B	C	D
2	These are apartments.	A	B	C	D
3	In this photo there is a ladder.	A	B	C	D
4	This property has big white gates at the entrance.	A	B	C	D
5	This home has a garage.	A	B	C	D
6	The garden has lots of furniture in it.	A	B	C	D
7	This property has a clothes line on the balcony.	A	B	C	D
8	This home has lights in the garden.	A	B	C	D
9	This property has a white front door in the centre of the house.	A	B	C	D
10	The garden has a barbecue.	A	B	C	D
11	This property has a large, natural roof.	A	B	C	D
12	On the right of the house there is a path to the front door.	A	B	C	D

Speaking

PART 1

Listen and answer the questions about house and home.

1 Where do you live?

2 Who do you live with?

3 What sort of home do you live in?

Speaking tip

In Speaking Part 1, you will be asked general questions about yourself. These often include your name, age, where you live, who you live with, daily routines and things you like or don't like. Be prepared! Learn some responses to everyday questions about yourself.

Reading

For each question, choose the correct answer.

1

Need a cleaner?
Experienced cleaner happy
to do most things around
the home, for example, wash
clothes, take out the rubbish
and clean the windows.
Won't disturb you!
Call Denise
465465772

A   Denise needs a cleaner.

B   Denise has worked as a cleaner before.

C   Denise won't empty the bins.

2

Hi Mr Hale,
Just to let you
know I can finish
repairing your
roof on Thursday.
Let me know if
this is OK for
you.
Bill

A   Bill repaired Mr Hale's roof on Thursday.

B   Bill won't finish repairing Mr Hale's roof.

C   Bill hasn't finished repairing Mr Hale's roof.

3

HOME FOR SALE

Very interesting property
available to buy in your area!
This home, which is in the
centre of town next to the
town hall, used to be a
cinema.
Call Bella to make an
appointment!
899078613

A   Bella is interested in visiting a home that is for sale.

B   The home that is for sale was once a cinema.

C   A cinema, which was a house before, is for sale.

Reading tip

In Reading Part 1, read the text and
decide what the situation is. Use the visual
layout to help you decide if it is a text
message, an email, a note, a notice, etc.
Decide who has written the text and why.

Grammar: **Relative pronouns: *who, which, that, whom, whose***
Use to introduce relative clauses without repeating the
person or thing being referred to.

This home, *which* is in the centre of town next to the town hall, used to be a cinema.

Choose the correct relative pronoun to complete each sentence.

1   I live in an old house *whose / which* was built in 1900.

2   That's the famous footballer *who / whose* lives near me.

3   Where's the sofa *that / whose* was in your living room?

4   Ms Patel, *whose / that* house my parents bought, is my maths teacher.

Listening

For each question, choose the correct answer.

14 **You will hear a radio interview with a young girl called Molly, who likes animals.**

1 **Molly's first pet was**

   A a goat.

   B a cow.

   C a rabbit.

2 **Molly's got a lot of pets because**

   A her parents buy them for her as presents.

   B she takes the pets that her friends can't keep.

   C she finds animals that are on the streets.

3 **Molly's mum didn't want the pets in**

   A Molly's bedroom.

   B the dining room.

   C the garage.

4 **Molly thinks looking after pets**

   A isn't hard work.

   B is easy to do.

   C stops her doing some things.

Writing

Your English teacher has asked you to write a story.

Your story must begin with this sentence.

It was dark as I walked up the path to the front door, which was open!

Write your story in about 100 words.

writing tip

In Writing Part 3, use adverbs of manner to make your story more interesting.

For example, you could use: *quietly, loudly, slowly, quickly, carefully.*

I walked *slowly* towards the door.

Vocabulary

1 Complete the words.

1

je _ _ _ _ s

2

mis _ _ _ b _ _

3

p _ ti _ _ t

4

g _ _ _ rous

5

cu _ _

6

ash _ _ _ _

7

a _ x _ _ _ _

8

bo_ _ _

9

del _ _ h _ _ _

Grammar: *–ed* and *–ing* adjectives

Adjectives that end in *–ed* tell us how someone feels.
I'm bor*ed*.

Adjectives that end in *–ing* describe the thing that causes the feeling.
This film is bor*ing*.

Choose the correct options to complete the sentences.

Jane, please can you stop making that noise. It's very *annoying / annoyed* and I'm trying to do my homework. I'm really *annoying / annoyed*.

2 Write the correct ending of the adjective (–ed or –ing) to complete each sentence.

1 The new shopping mall in our town is *amaz*_____ – it's got four floors, a cinema and a swimming pool.

2 It's Kate's birthday tomorrow and she's very *excit*_____.

3 I'm really *interest*_____ in history and I love visiting old castles and palaces.

4 Walking home in the dark is *frighten*_____.

5 I don't really understand my English homework – the instructions are very *confus*_____.

6 I don't want to go to the park after school – it's *bor*_____.

7 I was really *embarrass*_____ at school today – my mum came into my class to give me my lunch because I'd left it at home!

8 Tara will be *disappoint*_____ that there are no tickets available for the cinema on Friday.

3 Choose the correct word from the box to complete each sentence.

> challenging   cheerful   cruel   gentle   reliable   rude   unusual

1 Our car isn't very _____ – it's always breaking down.

2 I like visiting my grandad because he's never sad. He's always very _____.

3 The 10 kilometre run was very _____ but I managed to finish it.

4 Benji is a big dog but he's very _____. When I play with him, he never hurts me.

5 In the story, the aunt is a _____ woman who puts the children in a cupboard and locks the door.

6 Oliver is a _____ boy who always talks when the teacher is talking.

7 May's house is _____ because the garden is on the roof.

Speaking

15

Here is a photograph. It shows a father and son at the weekend. Tell me what you can see in the photograph.

Speaking tip

In Speaking Part 2, describe the photo in as much detail as possible. Here are some ideas:

• weather (*It's a sunny day.*)

• clothing (*He's wearing…*)

• actions (*He's walking.*)

• prepositions of place (*He's walking next to a lake. There's a bridge over the river.*)

• feelings (*He looks sad.*)

For each question, choose the correct answer.

Write *one* word for each gap.

Yesterday evening
by Peter Harrington

I was watching a romantic film yesterday evening when my sister came into the living room. She picked up the remote control and changed the film to a horror film. I don't really like horror so I wasn't very happy. She told me that she really wanted to watch a film with me **(1)** _____ that she didn't like romantic films. I asked her if we **(2)** _____ watch a different film – one that we both liked, but she said no. As **(3)** _____ as the film started my sister insisted on turning all the lights off. Then she thought it was funny to shout 'Boo!' at me loudly. I said, 'If you do that again, I **(4)** _____ leave.' She just laughed. We didn't speak for a while. The film was very frightening and I was not having a good time. But in the end, it was **(5)** _____ a problem. I was thinking of a way to leave the room **(6)** _____ my sister suddenly turned off the TV. I looked at her – she was shaking. She was scared too! So we listened to some music instead.

Grammar: **Past continuous interrupted by past simple: to talk about actions in the past which were stopped or interrupted by another event**

past continuous   *past simple*

I *was watching* TV when the phone *rang*.

Choose the best options to complete the sentences.

1   George *ate / was eating* his dinner when the electricity *went / was going* off.

2   As I *ran / was running* in the park a dog *bit / was biting* me.

Note: we often use the words *when* or *as* to connect the two events.

Listening

16

For each question, choose the correct answer.

1   You will hear a father and son talking about a tennis match they have watched.

   The father thinks the players were

   A   exciting.

   B   awesome.

   C   slow.

2   You will hear a mum describing a new neighbour to her daughter, Jane.

   The mum thinks the neighbour is

   A   awful.

   B   cool.

   C   negative.

3   You will hear a boy, William, talking to his friend, Lucia, about his homework.

   What does William think about his model?

   A   It's exciting.

   B   It's very good.

   C   It's terrible.

> **Listening tip**
>
> In Listening Part 2, remember that you are likely to hear *all* the options in the audio recording. So, make sure you check your answer the second time you listen. Think about who says each key word, and if they are saying something negative or positive.

Writing

Your English teacher has asked you to write a story.

Your story must begin with this sentence.

I was reading a book in the garden when I heard a strange noise.

Write your story in about 100 words.

> **Writing tip**
>
> In Writing Part 3, remember that your story should have a beginning, a middle and an end.

Unit 7   Sport

Vocabulary

1 Listen and tick the correct photo.

1 A   B
  _____   _____

2 A   B
  _____   _____

3 A   B
  _____   _____

4 A   B
  _____   _____

5 A   B
  _____   _____

2 Write the sports under the photos in Exercise 1. Then listen and check.

3 Complete the missing words.

1 A person who does athletics is called an a_____.

2 A person who takes part in a competition is called a c_____.

3 A person who uses their hands to stop goals in a football match is called a g_____.

4 A person who cycles is called a c_____.

5 A person who wins a championship is called a c_____.

6 A person who rides a horse is called a r_____.

7 The place where you put on your sports clothes is called the c_____ r_____.

8 The place where you play football matches is called a football p_____.

9 The place where athletic competitions happen is called a s_____.

10 The place where you play tennis is called a c_____.

4 Look at the photo and decide if each sentence is true (T) or false (F). Correct the false sentences.

1 The photo shows the sport of motor racing.   T   F
_____

2 In this sport people drive cars around a pitch.   T   F
_____

3 Helmets must be worn by the competitors in this sport.   T   F
_____

4 This isn't an extreme sport.   T   F
_____

Grammar: **Modal passives: to talk about rules for sporting activities**

Helmets *must be worn* by competitors.

Choose a sport you like. Write a rule for the sport using a modal passive.

Possible modal verbs you could use: *should, can, could, needn't, need to, must.*

Speaking

PART 3

19

Some friends are going to the sports centre together. Here are some sports they could do there. Describe each of the sports and say which would/wouldn't be the most fun to do with friends and why.

Reading

Read the text about Elisa. For each question, choose the correct answer.

19-year-old Elisa Develin talks about her sporting career

Like most other little girls, I started ballet lessons when I was very young. I loved dancing, but I didn't really like ballet very much – it was too slow for me and the teacher wasn't very friendly. I cried when I had to perform on a stage in a show. My mum was a bit upset because she'd stayed up all night making my costume and she wanted to be one of those the proud mums who is watching their little girl in a ballet show. After that, I asked her if I could stop going to ballet classes, but she said I'd regret it if I did. I was annoyed with her and I never wanted to go to the classes. I remember arguing and shouting at her in the car on the way to the lessons; I didn't try very hard in the classes.

Then, one Saturday, I was at home with my dad and we were watching a sports programme on TV. It was a gymnastics competition. I remember thinking it was amazing. I immediately started doing gymnastics around the house. My dad realised I was better at gymnastics than ballet. He found a gymnastics coach for me, and I gave up dancing. I think Mum was a bit angry about it. Soon I started entering gymnastic competitions and winning them. I did feel a bit guilty about the arguments I used to have with my mum about ballet, because my gymnastics coach told me that ballet was really useful for gymnastics.

Unfortunately, a year ago I hurt my shoulder very badly. Although I still do gymnastics, I can't compete again. At first this made me very angry. I stopped going to training and I even stopped watching gymnastics on TV. But recently, I've realised how much I miss gymnastics, so I've decided to use my talent to teach other people. I now work with my coach as a gymnastics instructor and I'm really proud of the children I work with. When they win competitions, I feel so proud of them and it feels as if I'm winning too.

1 **Why did Elisa and her mum argue?**
   A Elisa didn't like the costume her mum made her for a ballet show.
   B Elisa's mum wanted her to give up ballet classes but Elisa didn't want to.
   C Elisa wanted to give up ballet lessons but her mum didn't want her to.
   D They were always late for ballet classes because her mum drove slowly.

2 **How did Elisa's parents feel about her giving up ballet to do gymnastics?**
   A Her dad supported her but her mum wasn't pleased about it.
   B They encouraged her to give up ballet and take up gymnastics instead.
   C They felt guilty she hadn't started gymnastics at a younger age.
   D They thought she should become an instructor.

3 **What might a journalist write about Elisa now?**
   A Elisa is very angry that she can't compete anymore, but hopes to help others to become champions.
   B Elisa didn't like competing, but she wants to continue working in gymnastics as an instructor.
   C Elisa is currently unable to compete in gymnastics competitions, but she hopes to be able to compete again in the future.
   D Although Elisa is unable to compete in the sport she loves, she is happy to share her experience with others.

Listening

 For each question, choose the correct answer.

20

1 Which sport did the girl do at school?

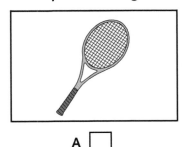

A ☐

B ☐

C ☐

2 What day is the badminton competition?

| MONDAY | TUESDAY | WEDNESDAY |

A ☐

B ☐

C ☐

3 Where is Curtis?

A ☐

B ☐

C ☐

Writing

PART 2

Write your answer in about 100 words.

You see this announcement in an English-language magazine.

Write your article.

ARTICLES WANTED
Write an article telling us what sports you and your friends enjoy doing and how often you do them.
Do you think it's important for teenagers to do sport? Why or why not?
The best articles answering these questions will be published next month.

> **writing tip**
> Try not to repeat key words. For example, instead of using *like* all the time to express your preferences, you could use *love*, *am keen on* or *enjoy*. This will make your writing more interesting.

33

Vocabulary

1 Complete the crossword.

Across

3 a person who works in a library

4 a person whose job is to care for people who are ill or injured

6 a person who is able to work but doesn't have a job is this

8 a person who looks after a child while the child's parents are not at home

9 a person who cooks in a restaurant

11 a teacher at a university or college

12 a person whose job is to collect news stories for newspapers, magazines, television or radio programmes

Down

1 someone who does work without being paid because they want to do it

2 the people who work on a ship or an aeroplane

4 a person who writes novels

5 someone whose job is to watch and protect a person, place or object

7 someone whose job is to discover what happened in a crime and to find the people who did the crime

8 someone who cuts up and sells meat

10 a member of an army

12 a person who decided how a criminal should be punished, or a person who decides the winner of a competition

2 Complete the text using the words from the boxes. There are **THREE** words you do not need.

> applying   full-time   guest   part-time   retiring
> salary   tour guide   volunteer

My grandad is sixty-five years old. He's been a travel agent for forty years, but he's **(1)** _____ next week. He doesn't want to stay at home all the time, but he doesn't want another job either. So he's going to be a **(2)** _____, showing people around the city and telling them about its history. It's a **(3)** _____ job, only working on Mondays and Wednesdays. He'll be a **(4)** _____, so he won't get a **(5)** _____, but he doesn't mind. He isn't starting for a month because he wants to have a holiday first.

Grammar: **Future with present continuous: to talk about future arrangements**

He *isn't starting* for a month.

Note: We use a time reference, for example, *next year, next month, on Tuesday, in 2030,* when we use the present continuous to talk about the future.

Answer these questions. Write full sentences.

1 What are you doing this weekend?

2 When are you taking your Preliminary English exam?

Speaking

PART 4

21

Listen and answer the questions about work and jobs.

1 Tell me about a job you'd like to do when you are older.

2 Would you like to work as a volunteer? Why or why not?

3 Do you think it's better to go to university or to get a job when you leave school?

4 Do you think teenagers should get part-time work? At what age?

5 What do you think are the advantages and disadvantages of working in an office?

Reading

For each question, write the correct letter (A–F) next to each number. There are two options you do not need to use.

The young people below are all looking for part-time jobs. Below there are advertisements for six part-time jobs. Decide which job each person would be the most suitable for.

1  Tilda is quite serious and finds it hard to talk to people. She prefers to play games on her computer, make videos and read books. When she grows up she wants to make video games. She'd like to get a job so that she can afford more video games and computer software. She's an only child, so she hasn't got any brothers or sisters and isn't used to being with younger children. She thinks it would be good to get a job where she has to talk to some people so that she can become more confident, but she doesn't want to have to talk to many people. ____

2  Simon hates sitting down and being quiet. He loves sports and the countryside. He often goes hiking with his parents at the weekend. He only wants a job that is outside. His grandparents give him lots of money every month, so he doesn't need a wage. ____

3  Grace is 14 years old. She'd like to get a job with her best friend Lisa. They don't mind what job they do, but they don't want to work at the weekends. They'd like to earn some money so that they can go shopping. ____

4  Josh is 13 years old. He'll be 14 in three months' time. He's got two younger brothers, so he's very good with younger children. He's very patient, kind and fun. He loves sports and art. He would like to have a part-time job and earn some money, but he does a lot of clubs after school, so he can only work at the weekends. ____

Part-time job advertisements

A   Babysitter needed
Mr Hunt is looking for a reliable student (boy or girl) aged 14+ to look after his children on Wednesday evenings. You should be happy to play with the children and be gentle and kind.

B   Beach cleaners wanted
Do you have some free time? Do you love our beach? Can you volunteer to help clean it? If you would like to volunteer, please join us every Sunday on the beach from 10.00 a.m. to 4.00 p.m. Lots of people are needed – bring your friends! ☺

C   Tennis instructor needed
The school sports department is looking for a student who is good at tennis to help coach children from the local primary school on a Saturday morning for two hours. You must be able to give clear instructions and be patient. Please only make an application if you are over 13.

D   Cleaners needed
The school art department will pay two students to tidy up and clean the art rooms together every day after school for half an hour. You don't have to be interested in art for this job.

E   Librarian wanted
The school library needs someone to come and help at lunchtimes please. Suitable candidates will be calm, polite and interested in books. You must be able to use a computer and help students who are visiting the library. The job starts next month.

F   Photographer needed
The school website needs a photographer to take 10–12 photos every month to upload to the website. You must find out what is going on in each department and at the school clubs. Talk to teachers and students about what they would like to see on the website. Download an application form from the website if you are interested in this job.

Listening

22

For each question, write the correct answer in the gap. Write *one* or *two words*, or a *number*, or a *date*, or a *time*.

You will hear a woman called Vicky Hunter talking about her job.

The best job in the world!

Vicky is a **(1)** _____.

She works with **(2)** _____.

She lives in **(3)** _____.

She has to be very **(4)** _____ in her job.

She's leaving her job on **(5)** _____.

Vicky would like to be a **(6)** _____ in the future.

Writing

Read this email from a hairdresser, Ollie, and the notes you have made.

From: Ollie the hairdresser
Subject: Your next appointment
Dear Jo, Thanks for your email. Yes, I can cut your hair. You can choose Friday this week or Monday next week. Which would you prefer? What time do you want to have your hair cut? In the morning, the afternoon or the evening? Can you please describe your hair to me? I'm looking forward to meeting you soon! Ollie

Great!

Tell Ollie choice and explain why

Suggest a time

Tell Ollie

Writing tip

In Writing Part 1, remember you must include all the prompts in your answer, and you must write your answer as an email.

Write your email to Ollie using all the notes.

Write your answer in about 100 words.

Vocabulary

1 Listen and write each word under the correct photo.

23

1

_____

2

_____

3

_____

4

_____

5

_____

6

_____

7

_____

8

_____

9

_____

2 Choose the correct word from the box to complete each sentence.

> hero   interval   interviewer   podcasts   scene   series

1 We went to see a play last night at the theatre. At the _____ Dad bought us all ice creams.

2 The _____ asked the politician some really good questions.

3 You should watch the new comedy _____ that's on Channel 6. It's amazing!

4 I did not like that film at all. The actors were awful and the _____ at the end of the film when the _____ died was too long. I was really bored!

5 I always take my headphones with me on the bus to school and I sometimes listen to music but usually I listen to _____.

3 Look at the photos. Match each sentence to a photo A, B or C.

	A	B	C

A   B   C

1	This is a music studio.	A	B	C
2	This is a TV talk show.	A	B	C
3	A band is recording a song.	A	B	C
4	The audience are watching a play.	A	B	C
5	The performers are on a stage.	A	B	C
6	A camera is recording the show.	A	B	C
7	There are musicians.	A	B	C
8	There are presenters.	A	B	C
9	There is a singer.	A	B	C
10	This is a theatre.	A	B	C
11	There are rows of seats.	A	B	C
12	There are actors.	A	B	C

Speaking

24

Here is a photograph. It shows a type of entertainment. Tell me what you can see in the photograph.

> **Speaking tip**
>
> In Speaking Part 2, describe where things are in the photo. You could use these words:
>
> *On the left/right*
>
> *In the background/ foreground/centre*
>
> *In front of the...*
>
> *there is/are...*
>
> *Behind the...*
>
> *Next to the...*

Reading

For each question, choose the correct answer.

1

Hi Pippa

Band practice tomorrow night at 6.30. Come to my house after school and we can go to Fiona's house together.

Becca

A Band practice is at Fiona's house.

B Band practice is at school.

C Pippa doesn't know where Fiona's house is.

2

SCHOOL PLAY

Can you help our actors? Excellent dance students needed to teach our actors a new dance for the school play.

A Dancers are needed to be in the school play.

B The play needs more actors.

C There will be dancing in the school play.

3

TalkingTimeTwo
TV chat show

Would you like to come to the TV studio, meet our cool presenters and their famous guests and watch us make the show?
Call Steve 9967584532

A The advert is for a TV chat show presenter.

B The advert is for audience members for a TV chat show.

C The advert is for guests for a TV chat show.

Listening

For each question, choose the correct answer.

25 **You will hear a radio interview with a young boy who goes to a special school.**

1 The children who go to Jack's school all want to be
   A stars.
   B talented.
   C actors.

2 For Jack primary school was
   A exciting.
   B boring.
   C fun.

3 The teacher from the entertainment school
   A spoke to Jack on the phone.
   B came to Jack's house.
   C called his parents.

4 Jack thinks entertainment school has
   A helped him improve in traditional subjects.
   B made him more confident.
   C made him famous.

> **Listening tip**
>
> In Listening Part 4, the text you will hear is long. It's important that you read the instructions and the questions carefully before you listen so you know what the topic is and who the speaker is.

Grammar: **Reported speech: to talk about what someone said, asked or commanded in the past**

	Direct speech	Reported speech
Statement	*I think he's* very good at acting.	*She said that she thought I was* very good at acting.
Question	*Would he like* to join my school?	*She asked them whether I* would like to join her school.
Question	*Do you like* your school?	*They asked me if I liked* my school.
Question	*Can I go* there?	*I asked if I could* go there.
Command	*Ask* him!	*She told them to ask* me.

Answer the questions. Write full sentences.
1 What did your English teacher say to you this week?
2 What did your mum or dad ask you this week?

Writing

Write your answer in about 100 words.

You see this advertisement in an online English magazine. **Write your review.**

> **REVIEWERS WANTED**
>
> Do you like watching and talking about TV series? Are you good at writing in English? We would like you to write a review of a TV series you have watched. Say what is good and what is bad about it and why. The best reviews will be posted in next month's magazine.

> **Writing tip**
>
> You could use these phrases in this writing task:
>
> *I recommend/don't recommend (watching)…*
>
> *It's the story of/about…*

41

Vocabulary

1 Listen and write each word under the correct photo.

26

1

_____

2

_____

3

_____

4

_____

5

_____

6

_____

7

_____

8

_____

9

_____

10

_____

11

_____

12

_____

2 Match the words to their definitions.

> blogger   chat room   data   homepage   invention
> password   podcast   ring   upload   volume

1 _____ : information that can be used by a computer program

2 _____ : a secret word or phrase you type in to a computer or phone in order to use it

3 _____ : how loud or quiet a sound is

4 _____ : a file containing a radio show or something similar that you can listen to on a computer or on an MP3 player

5 _____ : a website where people can exchange messages

6 _____ : to move a document, program, video or photo onto the internet

7 _____ : someone who writes about their thoughts or experiences online

8 _____ : the main page of a website (usually the first page you see when you go onto that website)

9 _____ : something that has been invented by someone

10 _____ : to phone someone and speak to them

3 Choose the correct words to complete the texts.

Yesterday, I was in town with my friend when I saw Tina Hunter, the famous
1 *podcast / blogger*. She writes one of my favourite **2** *blogs / homepages*, 'FoodFuss'.
On it she discusses what she eats and gives out recipes and even makes short
3 *text messages / video clips* that show you how to make each meal.

My friend really wants me to **4** *download / upload* a new **5** *app / social media* onto
my phone, but I'm not sure I should. The app allows you to take **6** *photos / podcasts*
and then draw on top of them to make them funny. Then you send them to your friends.
The problem is that you can't **7** *install / delete* them, so they will always be there online.

Speaking

PART 1

Listen and answer the questions about technology.

27

Speaking tip

Remember that for many questions you should use short form answers.
For example,
Yes, I do/No, I don't;
Yes, I can/No, I can't;
Yes, I have/No, I haven't

You can use *because* to add information to your answer.

Do you think smartphones should be allowed in school?

Yes, I do because *it's useful to take photos of the board on your phone in class so you can look at it again later when you are doing your homework.*

1 Do you have a mobile phone? Is it a smartphone?

2 Could you live without a smartphone? Why or why not?

3 Do you think smartphones should be allowed at school?

4 Do you use technology to help you learn English?

5 How do you use technology to communicate with your friends?

Reading

Read the text about 3D printing. For each gap, choose the correct option A, B, C or D.

3D printing

We did a really cool technology project at school last term. We designed a phone case and then learned how to print it using a 3D printer. The 3D printer was **1** _____ in the classroom. I had never seen one before. It looked very different from normal printers.

First, we had to use a special computer program to **2** _____ our phone cases. It was a little bit complicated, so we had to read the

3 _____ carefully. Then we transferred our designs to the 3D printer. Finally, the

4 _____ used plastic to create our designs in 3D.

The 3D printer we have at school is not very big, but the teacher showed us videos of 3D printers which are used in **5** _____ for printing things like car parts and furniture.

1 A switched off	**B** installed	**C** downloaded	**D** unpacked
2 A invent	**B** blog	**C** connect	**D** design
3 A answer	**B** message	**C** instructions	**D** advice
4 A machine	**B** mouse	**C** robot	**D** server
5 A industry	**B** school	**C** factory	**D** classrooms

Reading tip
In Reading Part 5, read the title and the text quickly to find out the topic and general meaning first. Then try to think about what word might fill each gap, e.g. a noun, verb or adjective, and if it is a noun whether it will be singular or plural.

Grammar: Past perfect

I had never seen one before!

We use past perfect to describe the past before another past.

(1st action in the past)   (2nd action in the past)

I had never seen a 3D printer before I saw one last term.

Answer the question. Write a full sentence.

Had you ever heard about 3D printing before you read this text?

Listening

For each question, choose the correct answer.

28

1 How did the girl finally contact her grandma?

A   B   C

2 What does the dad want for his birthday?

  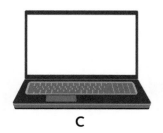

A   B   C

3 What isn't broken?

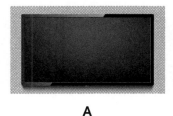  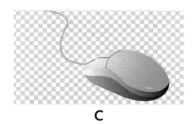

A   B   C

Writing

Write your answer in about 100 words.

You see this announcement on an English-language website.

TECHNOLOGY I COULDN'T LIVE WITHOUT!

We want to know what technology people aged 12–15 are using and why they love it.

If you are 12–15 and use technology often, write an article telling us what technology you couldn't live without and why.

How would your life be different if you didn't have this technology?

Check out the results on our website next month.

writing tip

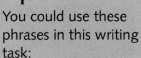

You could use these phrases in this writing task:

I couldn't live without … because

I use this technology every hour/day/week to …

If I didn't have … , I would/wouldn't …

Write your article.

Vocabulary

1 Listen and tick the correct photo.

29

1 A

☐
_____

B

☐
_____

2 A

☐
_____

B

☐
_____

3 A

☐
_____

B

☐
_____

4 A

☐
_____

B

☐
_____

5 A
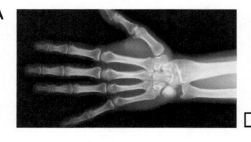
☐
_____

B
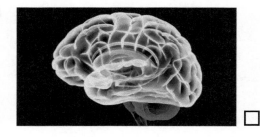
☐
_____

2 Write the words under the photos in Exercise 1. Then listen and check.

30

3 Complete the words.

1 h _ _ _

2 f _ _ _ _ _

3 _ n _ _

4 t _ _ s

5 f _ _ _

6 an _ _ _ _

7 _ ee _

8 _ _ g

4 Choose the correct words from the box to complete each sentence.

diet   emergency   painful   patients   prescription   sick

1 When Andy broke his arm it was very _____.

2 The doctor gave me a _____ for some medicine. I had to go to the chemist to collect it.

3 My mum and dad eat a very healthy _____ – they eat lots of fruit and vegetables, and they don't eat any sugar.

4 If you feel _____, you should go to the school nurse.

5 At the clinic there were lots of _____ waiting to see the doctor.

6 It was an _____, so Flo phoned for an ambulance.

Speaking

PART 2

31

Here is a photograph. It shows a father and son. Tell me what you can see in the photograph.

Reading

Read the text about toothache.

Five sentences have been removed from the text.

For each question, choose the correct answer.

There are three extra sentences which you do not need to use.

Toothache
By Sean, aged 12

I love chocolate and candies, biscuits and cakes – I love sugar! Mum and Dad have always told me to stop eating so many bad types of food. **(1)** _____ But I think it's OK, because I eat lots of healthy food like fruit and vegetables too. And I brush my teeth twice a day.

Unfortunately, I think they might be right. Two weeks ago, I woke up in the night because my tooth was very painful. I brushed my teeth, but my mouth still hurt. **(2)** _____ In the morning, it wasn't painful until I ate some toast for breakfast. Then it really hurt. **(3)** _____ I couldn't concentrate in the lessons because I had toothache and I couldn't eat at lunchtime. I felt miserable all day. When I got home, Dad took me to see the dentist. **(4)** _____ So now I'm having my tooth taken out on Saturday instead of going to a football match with my family. **(5)** _____ I'm also really sad about it because at the match I always have a big packet of sweets!

A So I told my mum, and she gave me some aspirin.

B I'm really scared about the operation – I think it might hurt!

C I didn't want to go to school but my parents insisted.

D He said that if I buy a new toothbrush, my tooth will be OK.

E I fell and broke my tooth.

F They say my diet isn't very healthy and that it is bad for my teeth.

G It's really important to look after your teeth.

H He said that my tooth was weak because I had eaten too much sugar.

Reading tip
In Reading Part 4, it's important that you read the whole text so that you understand who the writer is, what they are writing about and their attitude or opinion, before you try to complete the gaps.

Grammar: Causative *have*: to talk about something that someone else does for us or another person

have + object + *past participle*

So now I*'m having* my tooth *taken out* on Saturday.

Answer the questions. Write full sentences.

1 Have you ever had a tooth taken out?

2 Are you having your hair cut today?

3 When was the last time you had your photo taken?

Listening

PART 3

For each question, write the correct answer in the gap. Write *one* or *two words*, or a *number*, or a *date*, or a *time*.

32

You will hear a girl named Kissy talking about an accident.

My accident

Kissy is **(1)** _____ years old.

Kissy was in accident **(2)** _____ months ago.

Kissy's **(3)** _____ phoned for an ambulance.

When the ambulance arrived, Kissy already had a **(4)** _____.

At the hospital the nurse didn't give Kissy any **(5)** _____ because the doctor said she needed to have an operation.

Kissy stayed in hospital for **(6)** _____.

Writing

PART 1

Read this email from the headteacher of your school, and the notes you have made.

From: The headteacher
Subject: A healthy school
Dear students,
I'd like to make our school a healthier place. I think this is important for all students. — *Great!*
I'd like us all to take some exercise together every day. We could do this either before or after school for 30 minutes. What would you prefer? — *Say your choice and explain why*
What types of exercise do you think we could do? — *Suggest some types of exercise*
We'd also like to offer healthy school meals in the canteen. Please can you suggest a healthy meal you would like to have for lunch at school? — *Suggest a healthy meal*
Please email me with your ideas.
Ms Whittard

Write your email to the headteacher using all the notes.

Write your answer in about 100 words.

Vocabulary

1 Complete the crossword.

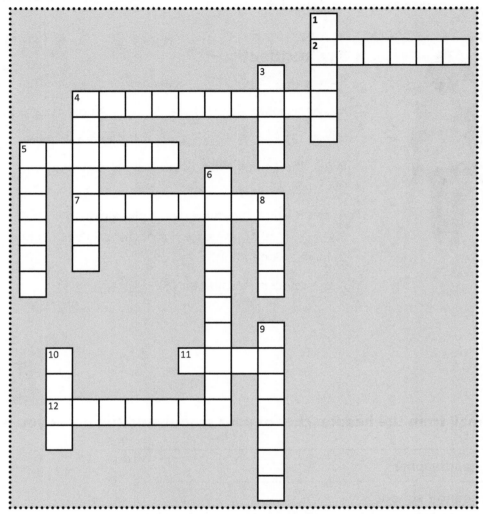

Across

2   a place where people work sitting at desks
4   a small hotel (two words, each 5 letters)
5   a very large house where a king, queen or president lives
7   the door or gate where you go into a place
11 a machine that carries people or things up and down inside a tall building
12 a large building where people use machines to make goods

Down

1   a tall narrow building or part of a larger building
3   a building that has some or all parts destroyed
4   a place where people go to look at art
5   a building where criminals are kept
6   a place where you can study after you leave school
8   the door that you use to leave a public building
9   a large sports pitch with rows of seats around it
10 a place where you can but drinks and small meals

Grammar: **Present simple passive: use it to talk about what a building is used for**

The verb *to be* + past participle

A building where criminals *are kept*.

Choose the correct words to complete the sentence.
A school is a place where students **(1)** *be / are* **(2)** *teach / taught* to speak English.

Now answer the question. Use the present simple passive. Write a complete sentence.
What is a bookshop?

50

2 Match each speaker (1–10) to the place they are going (A–J).

1 I'm going to my English class.
2 I'm going home to have a nice, warm shower.
3 I'm going to get my car fixed.
4 I'm taking my baby to see the doctor.
5 I'm buying some new sheets for my bed.
6 I'm going to get a map of the town.
7 I'm buying some eggs, milk and flour so that I can make a cake.
8 I'm buying Jane Clarkson's new novel for my grandma.
9 I'm taking back a book that I borrowed.
10 I'm going to check in.

A library
B apartment block
C hotel
D department store
E garage
F college
G grocery store
H tourist information centre
I bookshop
J clinic

Speaking

PART 4

Listen and answer the questions about buildings.

Speaking tip
In Speaking Part 4, remember
there are no right or wrong answers, so:
• talk about your personal experiences
• express your likes and dislikes
• share your opinions.

1 If you had to show someone around your town or city, which places would you take them to?

2 Tell me about the oldest building in your town.

3 Do you like to shop in department stores? Why or why not?

4 Do you think more teenagers go to bookshops or to libraries? Why?

5 Would you prefer to have a new stadium or a new shopping mall in your town or city? Why?

Reading

For each question, write the correct answer.

Write *one* word for each gap.

A city in the sky

The Shard tower is a modern building in the centre of London. It's made of glass. It has 95 floors, which makes it the tallest building in the UK. However, it is **(1)** _____ as tall as the Burj Khalifa building in the United Arab Emirates.

Originally the building was an office block with just 24 floors, but the tower that we see today was designed by the Italian architect Renzo Paino and it was built **(2)** _____ 1,450 workers **(3)** _____ 60 different countries.

Inside the Shard **(4)** _____ is a luxury hotel with a restaurant, gym and swimming pool on floors 34–52, apartments on floors 53–65 and offices on the other floors. There are also four restaurants in the building. And **(5)** _____ you don't want to walk up too many stairs, you can use one of the Shard's 36 lifts.

Grammar: **Past simple passive: use it to talk about the history of a building**

The verb *to be* in the past + past participle

*The tower we see today **was designed** by the Italian architect Renzo Paino.*

NOTE: When we say who did the action, we use *by*.

Choose the correct words to complete the question.

What building **(1)** *is/was* **(2)** *build/built* in your town or city last year?

Now answer the question. Use the past simple passive. Write a complete sentence.

Listening

For each question, choose the correct answer.

34

1 Where is the woman's car?

A ☐   B ☐   C ☐

2 Which shop has just opened in town?

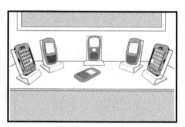

A ☐   B ☐   C ☐

3 Where are the friends going to meet?

A ☐   B ☐   C ☐

Writing

Write your answer in about 100 words.

You see this announcement in an English-language magazine.

Write your article.

al work
enence
t person

wanted for immediate start
Salary to reflect experience. 35 hrs p/w
Call our careers line now!

nescesa
friendly i
wanted fc
Outgoing
Full trainin

ARTICLES WANTED
Are you proud of the place where you live?
Write an article telling us what makes you proud of where you live.
What do you think would improve your town or city?
The best articles answering these questions will be published next month.

Email CV

R JOB!
USINESS
t individual
g package
828

WORK
No exper
Flexible h

CALL US
Opportu

Career

D
ividuals
te start
g given
5442

WANTED
Tempory teaching assistant wanted
Minimum 3 months / 30 Hrs p/w
ust have minimum of 3 years

NEW
Busy city
requires
Salary to
35 hrs p/w
be prenar

N
NCY!
rs p/w
vertime

Unit 13 Places: Countryside

Vocabulary

35

1 Listen and write the words in the correct places.

1 _____ 2 _____ 3 _____ 4 _____

5 _____ 6 _____ 7 _____

2 Look at the photo and decide if the sentences are true (T) or false (F).

1	This is a photo of the seaside.	T	F
2	This is a photo of a desert.	T	F
3	There are two waterfalls.	T	F
4	In the foreground there is a canal.	T	F
5	There is a valley in the mountains.	T	F
6	The lake is surrounded by fields.	T	F
7	The lake is in a forest.	T	F
8	There is a port at the end of the lake.	T	F

3 Match the words with their definitions.

canal   earth   land   port   region   scenery   stream   valley

1 _____: the substance in which plants grow

2 _____: a small narrow river

3 _____: a long narrow river made by people for boats to travel along

4 _____: a town by the sea where ships arrive and leave

5 _____: a low area of land between hills or mountains

6 _____: the land, water or plants that you can see around you in a country area

7 _____: an area of a country

8 _____: an area of ground, especially one that is used for a particular purpose such as farming

Speaking

PART 3

Joy and her family are going on holiday. Here are some places they could go. Describe each of the places and say which would be the most interesting to go to for a holiday.

Speaking tip

In Speaking Part 3, you will be discussing the pictures with another candidate.
Here are some phrases you can use to ask the other candidate what they think:
What do you think?   Do you agree?   What about you?

Reading

Read the text about the Grand Canyon.

For each question, choose the correct answer.

The Grand Canyon

The Grand Canyon is a large **(1)** _____ of natural park in the USA. Its extraordinary valley was made millions of years ago by the Colorado river, which runs through the park. It created both **(2)** _____ cliffs and big **(3)** _____ in the rock. The rock is famous for its beautiful colours.

Many people come to the park to go **(4)** _____ on the cliffs and exploring in the caves. Others come to go down the fast river on boats. There are many miles of hiking paths, too. For those people who are **(5)** _____ sporty, it is still possible to see the canyon, as there are helicopter rides over it.

The **(6)** _____ changes a lot throughout the year; during the winter it snows on the highest areas. In the summer it's very hot and there are often thunderstorms in August.

1	**A** area	**B** land	**C** earth	**D** island
2	**A** deep	**B** tasty	**C** steep	**D** soft
3	**A** harbours	**B** caves	**C** streams	**D** deserts
4	**A** looking	**B** driving	**C** flying	**D** climbing
5	**A** few	**B** less	**C** as	**D** either
6	**A** weather	**B** scenery	**C** rock	**D** idea

Grammar: **Prepositions of time:** *in, during* **+ months and seasons**

During the winter it snows on the highest areas.

In the summer it's very hot and there are often thunderstorms *in* August.

NOTE: use *the* after the preposition of time with seasons but not with months.

Write a sentence describing the weather in two different seasons or months in your country.

Listening

For each question, choose the correct answer.

37 **You will hear a radio interview with a woman called Kim.**

1 **Kim lives**
A in a city.
B in a village.
C on a farm.

2 **Kim believes that**
A children prefer the city to the countryside.
B teachers need holidays in the countryside.
C all children should visit the countryside.

3 **Activities on the farm include**
A walking, climbing and swimming.
B horse riding, walking and watching TV.
C horse riding, painting and swimming.

4 **Kim doesn't allow**
A shopping.
B mobile phones.
C fires.

Writing

Your English teacher has asked you to write a story.

Your story must begin with this sentence.

The boat moved slowly up and down on the sea.

Write your story in about 100 words.

Writing tip

In Writing Part 3, use different tenses to tell a story.

Use **past perfect** to say what happened before the story started.

I *had been* tired all week.

Use lots of short sentences in the **past simple** and write about problems. This will make your story more interesting!

I *couldn't…* / I *tried to … but* it *was* impossible.

Use **direct speech** with '…' and past simple forms: **asked** or **said**.

'Is everything OK?' the woman *asked*.

Vocabulary

1 Complete the words.

1 c _ _ _ m _ ch _ _ _

2 b _ _ _ _ op

3 cro _ _ r _ _ _ _

4 f _ _ n _ _ _ n

5 mo _ _ _ _ _ _

6 p _ v _ m _ _ _

7 s _ g _ _ _ _ t

8 _ _ _ wa _

9 _ unn _ _

10 ro _ _ _ ab _ _ _

11 _ _ _ _ _ _ st _ _ _ _ _

12 b _ _ _ _ _

2 Choose the correct words to complete the text.

My **(1)** *route / signpost* to school goes along my road, then over the **(2)** *turning / bridge* and into the park. If I'm early, I stop at the lake to feed the ducks. There's a big **(3)** *fountain / square* in the middle of the lake but it only works in the summer. When I come out of the park, I use the **(4)** *roundabout / crossing* to get across the busy road. I walk past the market and then turn left towards the town square. My school is at the end of the road on the **(5)** *corner / motorway* of the square.

3 Choose the correct words from the box to complete the conversation.

> airport   park   playground   square   underground   zoo

Leanne:	Hi Christy. Where shall we go on Saturday?
Christy:	Hmmm... I don't know. Shall we go for a walk in the **(1)** _____?
Leanne:	I'd rather not! There are too many people jogging there on a Saturday. What about the **(2)** _____? I think there's a new slide.
Christy:	No, the slide's broken and anyway we're a bit too old for that.
Leanne:	Oh! OK, let's go to the **(3)** _____ – we can watch the planes landing.
Christy:	That's boring. I'd prefer to go to the **(4)** _____. I love animals.
Leanne:	Do you know how much it costs? I think it's too expensive. Shall we go on the **(5)** _____? I like going on the trains.
Christy:	Maybe.
Leanne:	Oh, I know. There's a theatre show outside in the **(6)** _____. My sister says it's really good. We could watch that.
Christy:	Yes! That's a great idea. Let's do that.

Grammar: **Indirect questions: to ask polite questions**

Direct question: How much does it cost?

Indirect question: Do you know *how much it costs?*

Note: With indirect questions we use the word order of a normal positive sentence.

Change these direct questions into indirect questions. Start each question with the words given.

1 Where does Pritti live? *Can you tell me...*

2 What time does the booking office open? *Could you tell me...*

Speaking

PART 2

Here is a photograph. It shows a mother and son in a town. Tell me what you can see in the photograph.

38

For each question, choose the correct answer.

Write *one* word for each gap.

A visit to London
By Tara Jones

I'm really excited. Next weekend, my family and I **(1)** _____ going to London for the weekend. I **(2)** _____ never been before and there are so many things I want **(3)** _____ see and do.

The first thing we're **(4)** _____ to do is to visit Buckingham Palace, **(5)** _____ the queen lives.

Then I want to go to Covent Garden Market and buy lots of souvenirs for me and my friends.

My dad wants to visit the Tower of London and my mum wants to go to the Tate art gallery. **(6)** _____ there's time, we'll also go to London Zoo.

Reading tip In Reading Part 6, think about grammar and the meaning of the whole sentence and the whole text. Read the text once before you try to fill any gaps. Then read each sentence carefully and think of a word that makes sense in each gap. Then read the whole text again to check it makes sense.

Listening

For each question, choose the correct answer.

39 1 You will hear two friends talking about a new monument in their town.
      The boy says the monument is of
      A   an important person.
      B   someone from the town.
      C   a sports hero.

2 You will hear a woman asking a man for directions.
   What does the woman need to go through?
   A   the park
   B   the square
   C   the tunnel

3 You will hear a boy, Eddie, telling his friend about a recent trip to a city.
   Eddie thinks the city
   A   was easy to get around.
   B   has a great underground system.
   C   was too busy.

Grammar: **Embedded questions: a question that is inside a statement.**
Use to give more information about your opinion or attitude.

Direct question: Why did they decide to put up a statue of him?

Embedded question: I wonder why they decided to put up a statue of him. (extra information: the speaker is curious)

Note: When the embedded question is in a statement, use a full stop and not a question mark.

Change these direct questions into embedded questions. Start each question with the words given.
1   Where's my phone? *I don't know...*
2   Which way is it to the city centre? *I wonder...*

Writing

Read this email from your English penfriend, and the notes you have made.

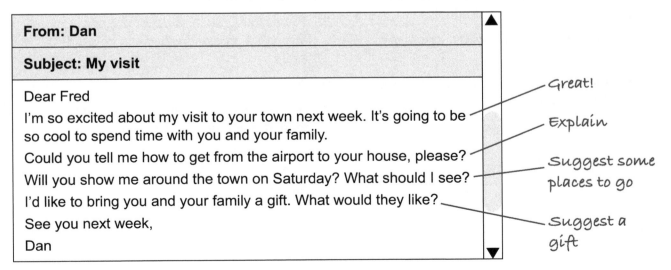

From: Dan

Subject: My visit

Dear Fred

I'm so excited about my visit to your town next week. It's going to be ⟶ *Great!*
so cool to spend time with you and your family.

Could you tell me how to get from the airport to your house, please? ⟶ *Explain*

Will you show me around the town on Saturday? What should I see? ⟶ *Suggest some places to go*

I'd like to bring you and your family a gift. What would they like? ⟶ *Suggest a gift*

See you next week,

Dan

Write your email to Dan using all the notes.

Write your answer in about 100 words.

Vocabulary

1   Complete the crossword.

Across

4   Changes in the Earth's climate because the planet is getting warmer (two words, 7 letters and 6 letters)

5   Someone who does work without being paid because they want to do it

6   The process of making water, air or land dirty and dangerous

8   A light but strong material used to make bottles and bags

Down

1   Paper or rubbish that people leave lying on the ground in public places

2   Fuel which you use in some cars and other vehicles to make them go

3   To put things such as paper or glass through a process so they can be used again

6   Illegal

7   All the vehicles that are on a particular road at one time

2 Match the photos to the correct texts. There is one text you do not need.

1

A You can see a lot of pollution in this photo. There's a traffic jam in the city and it's creating lots of smoke.

B There's a lot of smoke in this photo. It's going over the streets and the people are covering their faces because it's making them cough.

2

C The pollution in this photo is coming from the factories in the background. The smoke is going over the city and into the sky.

3 Choose the correct words from the box to complete the text.

bin   bottle bank   cans   cardboard   glass   recycling

On Saturday mornings, my dad and I do the **(1)**_____. We take all our
(2) _____, plastic **(3)** _____ and **(4)**_____ to the recycling bins.
Dad puts all the glass in the **(5)** _____ while I put all the other recycling in the
correct bins. We then put all our other rubbish in the rubbish **(6)** _____.

Speaking

PART 3

Some students are discussing the worst things a person can do for the environment. Here are some of their ideas. Discuss these things and say which is the worst.

40

Speaking tip

In Speaking Part 3, here are some useful phrases for discussing your opinions.

I think it's worse to… than to…

The worst thing you can do for the environment is…

Do you agree?

Don't you think that… ?

Reading

For each question, write the correct letter (A–F) next to each number. There are two options you do not need to use.

The young people below all want to do something to help fight climate change. Below there are advertisements for six activities they could do. Decide which activity each person would be the most suitable for.

1

Harry is 12 years old. He thinks the only way to fight climate change is to stop waste. He always recycles things. He never buys plastic and he never leaves the tap on when he brushes his teeth. He thinks a lot of his friends don't think about the things they do. He'd like to encourage them to change.

2

Simone is 12 years old. She is very angry about the problems of climate change, and she thinks that no one listens to children and their ideas. She thinks it's important to explain what you think and how you feel.

3

Giles is 13 years old. He is very sociable and loves doing activities in groups. He loves art and is very creative. He'd like to use these skills to do something with others to help the environment.

4

Rosie is 13 years old. She really wants to help the environment. She gets very cross when she sees people drop litter or waste electricity. She thinks some people don't understand how this is bad for the planet and that they need more information about it.

Be a volunteer!

A Keep our streets and parks clean!
Please make a poster to encourage people to put their rubbish in the bin or to take it home with them.

B Clean up our town!
We need lots of volunteers to pick up litter around town. If you would like to volunteer, please meet us every Saturday and Sunday in front of the police station at 10.30 a.m.

C Postmen and women needed!
Please help! Could you deliver letters about climate change to the houses in the streets near where you live? If you are 13 or older and want to help fight climate change, please call Simi on 08974502211

D Make a change!
Can you help? We need volunteers to make things out of recycled materials to sell at our summer fair. Making day is Sunday 24th May. The money will go to help fight climate change.

E Write a letter!
Help the planet! Write a letter to your local politician telling him or her how you feel about climate change. Write and send it today!

F Make your school climate-friendly!
Students needed to go around school turning off lights in empty classrooms and taps that are not being used in the bathrooms, and to give talks to other students about why these things are important.

For each question, choose the correct answer.

41 **You will hear a radio interview with a boy called Chris.**

1 **Chris has**

   A taken some amazing photos of the beach where he lives.

   B written an article about rubbish in the sea.

   C organised a beach clean-up.

2 **Chris thought that**

   A lots of people would be interested in his idea.

   B a small number of people would be interested in his idea.

   C parents and grandparents would be interested in his idea.

3 **Because of what he did, Chris is now**

   A making podcasts.

   B going on chat shows.

   C cleaning up the beach.

4 **Chris**

   A blames adults for climate change.

   B thinks everyone has to try and stop climate change.

   C believes it's impossible to stop climate change.

Grammar: ***unless*: use in a conditional sentence instead of *if… not*.**

Unless we all do something to help, the planet will just get worse and worse.
= *If* we *don't* all do something to help, the planet will just get worse and worse.

Complete the sentence with your own idea.
Unless more people _____, climate change will get worse.

Writing

PART 2

Write your answer in about 100 words.

You see this announcement in an online English-language magazine.

ARTICLES WANTED
The biggest problem
the planet has
Write an article telling us
what you think is the biggest
problem the planet has.
What can we do about
this problem?
The best articles answering
these questions will be
published next month.

WANTED

writing tip

In Writing Part 2, your first sentence should clearly tell the reader what your writing is about. Usually, the first line of the advertisement or announcement will help you to write your first sentence.

For example: Write an article telling us what you think is the biggest problem the planet has?

Start your article with:

I think the biggest problem the planet has is…

Write your article.

Vocabulary

1 Listen and write each word under the correct photo.

42

1

_____

2

_____

3

_____

4

_____

5

_____

6

_____

7

_____

8

_____

9

_____

10

_____

11

_____

12

_____

2 Choose the correct word from the box to complete each sentence.

> bargain   damaged   exchange   expensive   ordered   reduced
> reserve   return   second-hand   shopping   spend   try on

1   Katie wants me to go shopping with her on Saturday because her grandma has given her 100 dollars to _____ on clothes.

2   I haven't got enough money with me to buy this dress now, but can I _____ it and come back tomorrow to buy it?

3   My sister never buys anything new. She says she prefers to buy _____ clothes.

4   Henry bought three T-shirts for £6. They were so cheap. What a _____!

5   Polly didn't _____ the shorts in the shop and they are too big. She'll have to take them back to the shop and _____ them.

6   Calvin never goes _____ – he thinks it's boring! He buys all his clothes online.

7   My mum's just _____ me a new bed online. It's coming next week.

8   The new shoe shop in the mall is more _____ than the shoe shop in town. You can get the same shoes for £8 less in town.

9   Customer: 'Excuse me. I'd like to return this top, please.'

   Assistant: 'Of course. What's the problem?'

   Customer: 'It's _____ – there's a hole in it.'

   Assistant: 'I'm very sorry. Would you like to _____ it for the same top, or would you like your money back?'

10   I'm so excited. The skirt I wanted is _____. It's down from $40 to $20! I'm going to buy it after school today.

Speaking

PART 4

Listen and answer the questions about shopping.

43

1   How often do you go shopping?

2   What do you like to buy?

3   Tell me about something you have bought recently.

4   Who do you prefer to go shopping with? Why?

5   What do you think are the advantages and disadvantages of shopping online?

Reading

Read the text about the Emperor's Market.

For each question, choose the correct answer.

The Emperor's Market

Few people know that the first shopping **(1)** _____ was built nearly 2,000 years ago. It was built by Emperor Trajan in Rome, Italy, and was called the Emperor's Market. It was a large building on several **(2)** _____ and it had a big impressive roof. Inside, there were approximately 150 shops on the lower floors selling lots of different products, such as silks, spices, food and **(3)** _____ clothing. The shops all had big windows where the shop owners put some examples of their goods so that the **(4)** _____ could walk around and see what was for **(5)** _____ in each shop. But the market had a lot more than just shops. On the top floors there was a library, places to eat and drink and the Emperor's offices.

1	**A** advertisement	**B**	assistant	**C**	customer	**D**	mall
2	**A** walls	**B**	floors	**C**	grounds	**D**	places
3	**A** luxury	**B**	satisfied	**C**	sweet	**D**	sharp
4	**A** customers	**B**	actors	**C**	soldiers	**D**	employees
5	**A** take	**B**	buy	**C**	sale	**D**	sell

Grammar: Quantifiers: *few, a lot of, many, some, any, lots of, a little* **Use to talk about quantities, amounts or degrees.**

Few people know…

Inside, there were approximately 150 shops on the lower floors selling *lots of* different products.

Write a paragraph about a day out shopping. Include three quantifiers.

Listening

For each question, choose the correct answer.

44

1 How much will the shop assistant sell the chair for?

£60	£72	£80

A ☐   B ☐   C ☐

2 Which item is the man selling?

 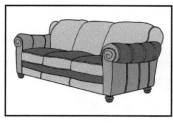 

A ☐   B ☐   C ☐

3 How much does the camera in the shop cost?

£80	£95	£125

A ☐   B ☐   C ☐

Listening tip

In Listening Part 1, look at the pictures and think about what topic you might hear.
For example, if you see three prices, then you will probably hear someone talking about buying or selling something. Think about the words you might hear in the conversation, e.g. *cost, price, dollars/euros/pounds, expensive, cheap...*

Writing

Write your answer in about 100 words.

You see this advertisement in an English-language magazine.

Write your article.

How important is shopping to you?

Could you live without shops?
How often do you go shopping?
How often do you buy things? Why?
Write us an article telling us about
your shopping habits and if
shopping is important to you.
The best articles will be published
in next month's magazine.

Unit 17 Weather

Vocabulary

1 Complete the words.

1

l _ _ _ _ n _ _ g

2

s _ _ s _ _ _ _

3

g _ _ e

4

_ _ y

5

fo _ _ _ _ _ _

6

t _ mp _ _ _ _ u _ e

2 Match the words with their definitions.

> breeze cool dry frozen humid mild shower
> storm thunder wet

1 _____ : wet and warm weather

2 _____ : the ground is hard because the weather is so cold

3 _____ : not too hot and not too cold

4 _____ : without any rain

5 _____ : a gentle wind

6 _____ : a short period of rain

7 _____ : having a low temperature, but not cold

8 _____ : very bad weather, with heavy rain and strong winds

9 _____ : raining

10 _____ : the loud noise that you sometimes hear from the sky during a storm

3 Complete the questions to match the answers.

1
How do we measure _____?

In degrees.

2
Was there a lot of _____ last night?

Yes, at least 10 cm – it should be enough to go skiing.

3
Do you like the _____?

No, I don't. I don't like to be too hot. I like mild weather.

4
What's the _____ like?

The wind is blowing quite hard – I think there may be a storm coming.

5
What's a _____?

It's a storm with thunder and lightning.

6
Why are the _____ so big and grey?

Because it's going to rain.

7
Is there _____ on the roads?

Yes, and there's a lot of snow too. It's quite dangerous to drive tonight.

8
Did you get _____ walking home today?

No, it was dry when I was walking and then it rained when I got into the house.

Speaking

PART 2

45

Here is a photograph. It shows a woman going home. Tell me what you can see in the photograph.

Speaking tip

In Speaking Part 2, imagine you are describing the photo to someone who can't see it.

Reading

For each question, choose the correct answer.

Write *one* word for each gap.

Growing grapes
By Ben Poynes

My family owns a grape farm. We watch the weather forecasts every week as grapes need the right weather (1) _____ grow. You plant grapes in the autumn when it's sunny. Grape plants love sunny weather, however, they also quite like it to be cold in the winter and warm in the growing season, (2) _____ is between March and April. The temperature needs to be above 10° centigrade during the growing season.

As (3) _____ as sunshine, grapes also need a lot of water. (4) _____ it doesn't rain for a long time, then we have to water the plants a lot. We must also think about the wind. If the wind is very strong, the ground becomes very dry and then we need to water the grapes.

In the winter we have to protect the grapes from frost, (5) _____ we put material over (6) _____.

Grammar: Modals: to express obligation

The temperature *needs to* be above 10° centigrade.

We *have to* water the plants.

We *must* also think about the wind.

Answer the questions. Write full sentences.

1 Do you have to look after any plants or animals? What do you have to do?

2 Do you need to do any homework after school today?

3 Where must you go when you get to school in the mornings?

Listening

 For each question, choose the correct answer.

46 **1** You will hear two friends talking about a hike they went on last Saturday.
   What was the weather like?

   A sunny and cool

   B mild with a few showers

   C wet with storms

2 You will hear a mother and son talking about the weather.
   Why can't the boy go to school?

   A Because it's too cold.

   B Because it's too windy.

   C Because it's snowing.

3 You will hear a man and woman planning a holiday.
   Where does the woman like to travel to in the winter?

   A To places that are foggy and cold.

   B To places that have snow.

   C To places that are hot and sunny.

Writing

Your English teacher has asked you to write a story.

Your story must begin with this sentence.

As soon as Tim's plane landed, he realised he had brought the wrong clothes.

Write your story in about 100 words.

 Writing tip

In Writing Part 3, make sure that you write your story using the first (I) or third (He/She/It) person to match the beginning sentence. So if the sentence you are given says *As soon as **Tim's** plane landed, **he** realised **he** had...* then you know you should continue the story in the third person.

Vocabulary

1 Listen and tick the correct photo.

47

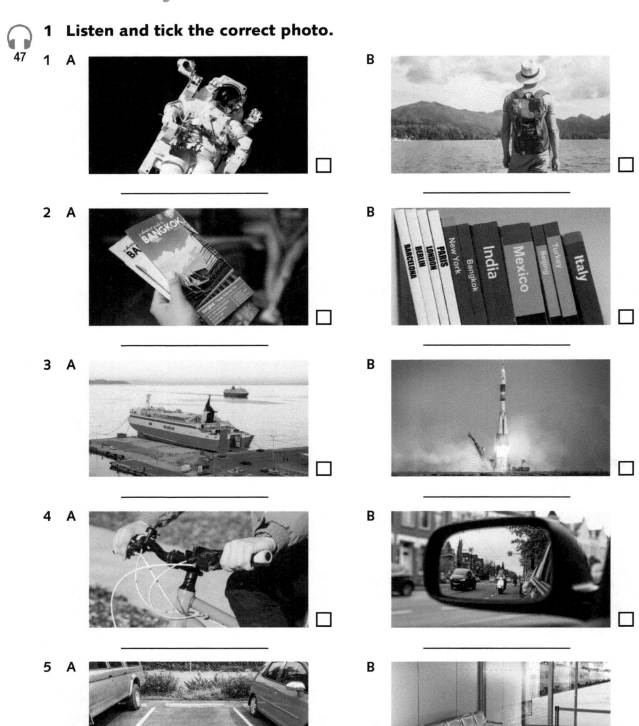

1 A ☐ _____

B ☐ _____

2 A ☐ _____

B ☐ _____

3 A ☐ _____

B ☐ _____

4 A ☐ _____

B ☐ _____

5 A ☐ _____

B ☐ _____

2 Write the words under the photos in Exercise 1. Then listen and check.

48

3 Write the words in the correct columns in the table.

air board business foot holiday land rail road sea time

by...		on...	

Speaking

49

Some students are discussing ways to travel around town. Here are some of their ideas. Discuss these things and say which is the best.

Speaking tip

In Speaking Part 3, remember that you will be discussing the photos with another student. Here are some useful phrases to use to respond to what the other student says.

I agree/disagree (because...).

That's true, however...

That's a good point/idea.

Reading

Read the text about a helicopter ride.

Five sentences have been removed from the text.

For each question, choose the correct answer.

There are three extra sentences which you do not need to use.

Denali National Park, USA
By Leila, aged 12

I've just had the best holiday ever in Alaska, USA. **(1)** _____ There aren't many towns or cities, but there's lots of countryside and lots of snow. The most exciting thing we did was to go on a helicopter ride over the Denali National Park. I'd never been in a helicopter before, and I was terrified. My sister's never liked flying so she refused to come. **(2)** _____ The pilot was very friendly and advised me to sit by the window. **(3)** _____ I soon forgot about being nervous.

On the flight we saw rivers and forests – and a lot of snow. There were no towns or villages for miles and miles. We didn't see anybody on the ground below. I felt like a real explorer. We flew around Alaska's tallest mountain – Mount McKinley – for a while. Then the helicopter landed on the ice. **(4)** _____ It was so much fun.

Then, on the way back to the airport, we were very lucky because we saw a brown bear on the snow below. **(5)** _____ .

A As soon as we took off, I understood why – the scenery was absolutely amazing!

B It's a pity, because it was definitely the best thing I've ever done.

C I've always wanted to be a helicopter pilot.

D Apparently, they are scared by the noise of the helicopter so it's quite rare to see them.

E It was so long and I felt tired.

F We got out and had a snowball fight with the other passengers and the pilot.

G Alaska is in the north of North America.

H However, the noise from the helicopter engine hurt my ears a lot.

Grammar: **Present perfect with *just*: to talk about something that happened a short time before now**

I've *just had* the best holiday ever in Alaska, USA.
Answer the question. Write a full sentence.
What have you just done?

Reading tip

In Reading Part 4, ask yourself questions to help you find the connections.

Read these key words and check if there are links to the text, or not.

As soon as we took off, I understood **why**… (why **what**?)

Apparently, **they** are scared by the noise. (**who**?)

We got **out** and had a snowball fight (out *of* **what**?)

It was so long and I felt tired. (**what** was so long?)

76

Listening

50

For each question, write the correct answer in the gap. Write *one* or *two words*, or a *number*, or a *date*, or a *time*.

You will hear a boy named Charlie talking about a journey.

My journey

Charlie is **(1)** _____ years old.

He's just been to **(2)** _____.

He travelled by **(3)** _____.

The journey took **(4)** _____ hours.

They departed from London at 9.15 p.m. and arrived in Fort William at **(5)** _____ the next day.

For dinner, Charlie had **(6)** _____ and potatoes.

Grammar: **Present perfect with *already*: to talk about something that happened earlier than expected or before something else**

We've *already booked* another one.

Answer the question. Write a full sentence.

What film does a friend or family member want to see that you've already seen?

Writing

Write your answer in about 100 words.

You see this announcement in an English-language magazine.

Write your article.

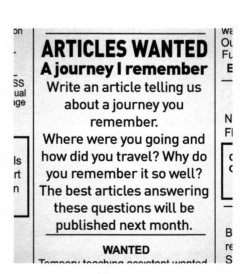

ARTICLES WANTED
A journey I remember
Write an article telling us about a journey you remember.
Where were you going and how did you travel? Why do you remember it so well?
The best articles answering these questions will be published next month.

WANTED

Vocabulary

1 Complete the crossword.

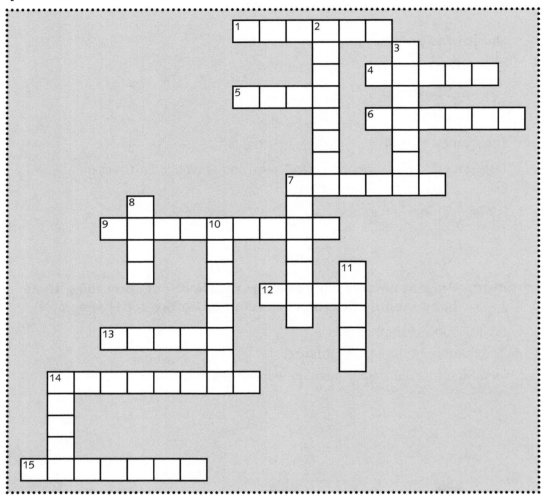

Across

1

4

5

6

7

9

12

13

14

15

Down

2  3  7  8

10  11  14

2 Complete the texts with the correct form of words from the box. Some answers are plural.

> branch   bush   continent   ice   leaf   moon   planet
> sky   species   star

We live on Earth. Earth is a **(1)** _____. When we look at the
(2) _____ at night, we can see the **(3)** _____. In the daytime,
we can see the sun. The sun is an enormous **(4)** _____.

A **(5)**_____ is a plant that is smaller than a tree. It has **(6)** _____
that grow on **(7)**_____. Many have flowers too.

The penguin is a **(8)**_____ of bird. Penguins live on the **(9)** _____
of Antarctica, which is covered in **(10)** _____ and is the coldest place on
the planet.

Speaking

PART 4

 Listen and answer the questions about the natural world.

51

1 What wildlife is there where you live?

2 What is your favourite season and why?

3 What is the countryside like where you live?

4 Have you ever been to the coast or to the mountains?
   Can you describe what it was like to me?

5 Do you think it's important to look after the natural world? Why or why not?

Reading

Read the text about Jade. For each question, choose the correct answer.

> ### 15-year-old Jade Jones writes about being a wildlife photography winner
>
> Although I've always loved animals, I only started taking photographs of them about two years ago. We were on holiday in Costa Rica and I saw some parrots in the rainforest. They were pulling seeds from the branches and I thought they looked funny, so I took some photos on my phone. Since then, I've taken photos of animals everywhere I go. While in the beginning my photos weren't that good, I think I'm improving. I take photos all the time. I chose to do photography as a subject at school and I think that's really helped me. I've been able to use lots of different cameras and to try out different techniques. Some people have suggested that I read books about photography or go to photo exhibitions but, while this may work for some young photographers, I don't think it would help me to improve because I think it's important for me to develop my own style.
>
> Whereas I'm not that proud of my first photos of the parrots, I'm really pleased with my photo that won the wildlife photography competition. It's of some birds that were living in my garden last winter. It shows the mother bird feeding her chicks. While I took the photo of the parrots in seconds, I had to wait a long time for this photo. I sat in the garden for nearly two hours waiting for the mother bird to come back with food. But I'm glad I did, because it's the best photo I've taken.

1   What does Jade think about her first photos of the parrots?

   A   They weren't very good.

   B   They were funny.

   C   They were better than the photos she'd taken previously.

   D   They were the best photos she's ever taken.

2   What is Jade doing to improve her photography?

   A   She's buying lots of different cameras.

   B   She's taking photography at school.

   C   She's going to lots of photography exhibitions.

   D   She's reading a lot of books about photography.

3   What might a journalist write about Jade?

   A   Although Jade is disappointed not to have won the photography competition, she is very talented and should not give up.

   B   Jade has a natural talent for taking photographs but unless she works harder, she is unlikely to succeed.

   C   Jade is a talented young photographer who needs to have more confidence in her work.

   D   Although Jade is still quite young her attitude to photography is excellent. She understands that you need to spend time and effort to get the most amazing photos.

Listening

 For each question, choose the correct answer.

52 1 **You will hear two friends talking about an island.**
What has happened on the island?

   A there's been a flood

   B there's been a fire

   C there's been a big wave

2 **You will hear two friends talking online.**
What season is it where the man is?

   A winter

   B summer

   C autumn

3 **You will hear a tour guide talking about some of the animals in her country.**
Which animal does the woman think is the most dangerous?

   A kangaroo

   B shark

   C mosquito

Writing

Your English teacher has asked you to write a story.

Your story must begin with this sentence.

Jane could see that the baby elephant was hurt.

Write your story in about 100 words.

writing tip

In Writing Part 3, use conjunctions in your writing. For example, *and, but, so, while, whereas, although.*

Vocabulary

1 Complete the crossword.

Clues

Across

6 a piece of writing or speech that has been put into a different language

7 to disagree with someone about something

8 the idea that a word or expression represents

9 to talk in an informal, friendly way

10 to say something about someone or something without giving too much information

Down

1 sharing information with other people for example, by speaking or writing

2 someone who has just started to do or to learn something

3 all the words in a language

4 the middle level, between two other levels

5 something that someone says to make you laugh

2 Choose the correct word to complete each question.

1 Can I **ask** / **say** you a question?

2 What does 'spectacular' **mean** / **tell**?

3 Could you send me the information in a (n) **letter** / **email** to my computer, please?

4 How do you **pronounce** / **speak** the word 'delicious'?

5 Can I **talk** / **ask** to you after the lesson, please?

6 Can anyone **answer** / **argue** this question?

7 What can you **tell** / **say** me about the UK?

8 Can you **speak** / **say** Russian?

9 Can you **translate** / **say** the poem into English for homework, please?

10 Did Mr Finch **mention** / **chat** anything about the test in class today?

Speaking

PART 3

Some students are discussing the best ways to practise a language. Here are some of their ideas. Discuss these things and say which is best.

Speaking tip

In Speaking Part 3, remember that although you must talk about all the pictures, you can also add your own ideas. So, for a topic about the best ways to learn a language, you could talk about how you like to learn English, even if there isn't a picture showing that.

Reading

For each question, choose the correct answer.

1
English conversation club

Are you worried about the advanced-level English speaking exams in March? Come to English conversation club starting in January. Intermediate-level club will begin in May after the spring break.

A   All students are welcome to the new English conversation club.

B   Intermediate level students have a speaking exam in March.

C   The club for advanced students will take place before spring break.

2
English-language Theatre Show – Friday afternoon

Don't forget to return your forms and payment to reception by Friday morning. People who have not paid will not be able to attend.

A   An English-language theatre group has been to the school.

B   An English-language theatre group is coming to the school.

C   There are no spaces left for people who want to see the English-language theatre group.

3

Hi Priya,
Could you please translate a message from my French penfriend for me? The grammar is really difficult and there's a lot of vocabulary I don't know.
Thanks
Greta

A   Greta needs help with her French homework.

B   Greta can't understand the meaning of a message in French.

C   Greta has translated a message in French for Priya.

Grammar: Prepositions following adjectives

Are you *worried about* the advanced-level English speaking exams in March?

Choose the correct prepositions to complete each sentence.

1   Jenny's really interested *in/ about / on* history.

2   I'm excited *on / by / in* the school trip to the USA next month.

3   I'm not very keen *for / on / about* Australian movies.

Listening

For each question, choose the correct answer.

54 **You will hear a podcast with a girl called Ruby.**

1 **Ruby**
   A   grew up hearing six languages at home.
   B   heard lots of different languages at school.
   C   lived abroad for six years.

2 **Ruby**
   A   finds listening to other languages difficult.
   B   likes telling jokes to her friends.
   C   mainly learned languages by hanging out with her friends.

3 **Ruby thinks it's important to be able to**
   A   read in another language.
   B   write in another language.
   C   teach friends another language.

4 **Ruby suggests that language learners should**
   A   make sure they don't make mistakes.
   B   try to communicate as much as possible.
   C   help others who are not as good as them.

Grammar: **Prepositions following nouns**

Do you have any *advice on* how to learn another language?

Prepositions following verbs

I sometimes get it wrong and then my friends *laugh at* me.

Choose the correct prepositions to complete each sentence.
1   This is an example *for / about / of* bad communication.
2   You clearly have a talent *for / by / with* languages.
3   Freya has had an argument *to / with / for* Aleisha.
4   I listen *of / for / to* podcasts in English to practise my listening skills.
5   I really couldn't concentrate *on / in / of* my work at school today.

Writing

Read this email from your English teacher Mr Thomas, and the notes you have made.

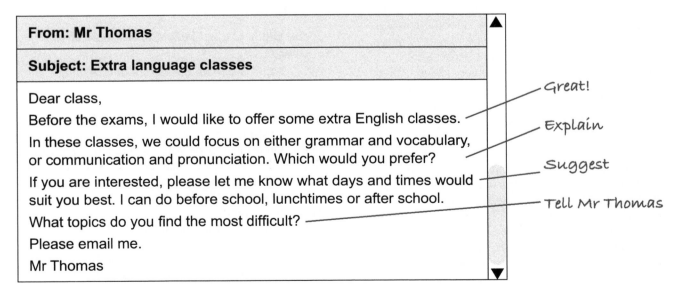

From: Mr Thomas

Subject: Extra language classes

Dear class,

Before the exams, I would like to offer some extra English classes. — *Great!*

In these classes, we could focus on either grammar and vocabulary, or communication and pronunciation. Which would you prefer? — *Explain*

Suggest

If you are interested, please let me know what days and times would suit you best. I can do before school, lunchtimes or after school. — *Tell Mr Thomas*

What topics do you find the most difficult?

Please email me.

Mr Thomas

Write your email to Mr Thomas using all the notes.

Write your answer in about 100 words.

Audio scripts

Unit 1 Clothes and accessories

Speaking
Track 1

1 Listen and write each word under the correct photo.

backpack, bracelet, earring, dress, glasses, handbag, necklace, perfume, raincoat, ring, socks, tracksuit

Speaking
Track 2

Listen and answer the questions about clothes and accessories.

1 Tell me about the clothes you like.
2 How often do you buy new clothes? Where do you buy them from?
3 Do you wear a uniform to school?
4 Do you like to wear the same clothes as your friends? Why or why not?
5 What jewellery do you wear most days? What accessories do you carry most days?

Listening
Track 3

For each question, write the correct answer in the gap. Write one or two words, or a number, or a date, or a time.

You will hear a woman called Kitty Hall telling a group of students about her work as a fashion designer.

Thank you for having me here today. I'm Kitty Hall and I've been a fashion designer for ten years. When I was 15 and still at school, I got a Saturday job in a clothes shop. That's when I fell in love with fashion. I wasn't particularly good at school and I didn't enjoy school that much, but I really liked working in the clothes shop. So, I left school when I was 16 years old and worked there full time. I became the manager at the age of 18 – I'm very proud of that. But when I was 21, I realised that I wanted to be more creative, so I left my job and went to college to study fashion design.

My first job after college was with a big fashion company as junior designer. I loved it and I learned a lot. I designed jeans for that company. Then, I got another job designing shoes. That was really cool! And two years later, I decided I was ready to start my own fashion company. It's called Dangle K and I mainly design and sell accessories. I love designing bags and jewellery, of course, but my favourite is belts. I think the right one makes an outfit look amazing and a belt really shows your personality! I've designed about 100 so far and I'm designing 20 new ones for Paris fashion week in the spring. It's very exciting! Now are there any questions?

Unit 2 Education

Vocabulary
Track 4

1 Listen and tick the correct photo.

1 rubber 2 library 3 pupil 4 pencil case 5 art lesson

Track 5

2 Write the words under the photos in Exercise 1. Then listen and check.

1 A ruler B rubber   2 A library B classroom
3 A pupil B teacher   4 A pencil case B dictionary
5 A music lesson B art lesson

Speaking
Track 6

Here is a photograph. It shows some children at school. Tell me what you can see in the photograph.

Listening
Track 7

For each question, choose the correct answer.

1 You will hear two friends talking about homework.

Boy: Our English teacher says he finds it difficult to read our handwriting so he's asked us to write our essays on a computer, but I'm not sure it's a good idea for me.
Girl: Computers are great for finding out information, but my history teacher said the same thing, so I wrote an essay on the computer and it took me ages. I'm very slow at typing and I made loads of mistakes.
Boy: I can't type at all! I think I'll ask if I can write my essay by hand.

2 You will hear a girl talking to her mum about college.

Girl: Mum, we were talking about college at school today.
Mum: Oh yes?
Girl: Yes, and I think I know what subjects I'd like to study when I go to college.
Mum: Great! I suppose you'd like to study French.
Girl: I do really like French, and I do want to study a foreign language, but actually I think if I go to college, I'll study Spanish.
Mum: I see. What else?
Girl: I'm thinking about studying art and history, too.
Mum: But you're better at geography than history.
Girl: Yes, you're right, and I do like geography but I prefer history.

Unit 3 Food and drink

Speaking

Track 8

Some students are having an end-of-term meal together. Here are some meals they are having. Describe each of the meals and say which would be most fun.

Listening

Track 9

For each question, choose the correct answer.

1 What did the boy buy from the supermarket?

Mum: Did you remember the shopping, Michael?
Michael: Well, I've bought the eggs. Here you are, Mum.
Mum: What about the loaf of bread?
Michael: I didn't have enough money. If you give me some more, I'll go back and get it, and the milk as well.

2 What is the man going to have for lunch?

Woman: Shall I meet you for lunch, James?
Man: Good idea. We could try that new café in town. I've heard they make lovely sandwiches.
Woman: I'd like a bowl of soup for lunch. I hope they have some.
Man: I'm sure they do. And I'm going to have one of their pizzas. Well, see you at lunchtime.

3 Which fruit mustn't the boy eat?

Boy: Mum? Can I have something to eat?
Woman: It will be dinner soon so I don't want you eating too much. Why don't you have some fruit? There are some apples in the kitchen. Go and get one. You'll see a box of strawberries out there as well but don't touch them, please. I need them for a cake. Or there are some bananas. Why not eat one of them?

Unit 4 Hobbies and leisure

Speaking

Track 10

Listen and answer the questions about hobbies and leisure.

1 What do you like to do in your free time?
2 What do you think are the best hobbies or leisure activities for children your age?
3 Tell me about a hobby you'd like to do. Think of something you have never done.
4 Where do you like to hang out with your friends? Why?

5 What do you think the advantages and disadvantages are of being a member of a club?

Listening

Track 11

For each question, write the correct answer in the gap. Write one or two words, or a number, or a date, or a time.

You will hear a woman called Lucy Jonson talking about her favourite hobby.

Hi, I'm Lucy Jonson and today I'd like to talk to you all about my favourite hobby. I live in a small village in the countryside. It's very beautiful – there are lots of fields and a big river. I love it! If I lived in the city, I'd go out with my friends to restaurants or to the cinema in the evenings or go shopping at the weekends, but because I live here, I go for walks instead. And when I walk, I think a lot and I have lots of ideas for stories. In the summer I sit in the fields or next to the river for hours, just thinking about good stories. I always take a notebook and a pencil with me and I write down any interesting thoughts or ideas. Then, when I get home, I make myself a cup of coffee, put some music on the radio, get my laptop out, sit at my kitchen table and write my stories. Sometimes, I can sit and write for six hours at a time. It gets dark outside and I haven't even noticed! I stop writing and realise that I'm hungry – I haven't had lunch and it's already dinner time. Writing stories makes me so happy – it's absolutely my favourite hobby. It's so creative and so much fun.

One of my stories has been made into a book. You can buy it in the shops. It's a story for small children and it's called *Honey Cake*! It's got beautiful drawings in it, but I didn't draw them. When I'm out on my walks I often make little drawings of things I see or imagine, but I'm not very good at drawing and I definitely couldn't put those pictures in a book.

Unit 5 House and home

Vocabulary

Track 12

1 Listen and write the words in the correct places.

mug, bowl, oven, sink, ceiling, drawer, bulb, cupboard, fridge, microwave

Speaking

Track 13

Listen and answer the questions about house and home.

1 Where do you live?
2 Who do you live with?
3 What sort of home do you live in?

Listening

Track 14

For each question, choose the correct answer.

You will hear a radio interview with a young girl called Molly, who likes animals.

Interviewer: Hi Molly. Thanks for coming on our programme today. When did you get your first pet and what was it?

Molly: Well, I've always liked to be around animals. My parents own a farm, so I've grown up with animals, you know, horses, goats, cows, but my first pet was actually a big grey rabbit. My parents gave him to me for my fourth birthday. They wanted him to live outside, but I said he had to live in my bedroom. My parents said he could, but that I couldn't have any more pets.

Interviewer: But you did get some more pets, didn't you? How did that happen?

Molly: Yes, I did. I had a friend who had some mice. She decided that she didn't want them anymore, so she asked me to have them. And I said yes. Then another friend moved to Australia and couldn't take her pet snakes with her. So, I had those too.

Interviewer: And it didn't stop there. You now have 40 pets in total, don't you?

Molly: Yes, I do. People just keep asking me to take their pets and I say yes.

Interviewer: And do they all live in your bedroom?

Molly: No. At first, they were all in my bedroom, but my bedroom isn't that big. I wanted to put some in the dining room, but my mum refused, so eventually my dad made the garage into a home for all my pets. He put in heating and lights, so it's very comfortable for them.

Interviewer: It must be hard work looking after all those pets…

Molly: Yes, definitely. It isn't easy. But I love them, so I don't mind, even if I can't go on holiday – because I can't leave them, you see.

Interviewer: And do you have a favourite pet?

Molly: Yes, it's still my first pet.

Unit 6 Personal feelings, opinions and experiences

Speaking

Track 15

Here is a photograph. It shows a father and son at the weekend. Tell me what you can see in the photograph.

Listening

Track 16

For each question, choose the correct answer.

1 You will hear a father and son talking about a tennis match they have watched.

Father: So, Liam, what did you think of the tennis match? It was exciting, wasn't it?

Liam: Ummm… well Dad, actually, I think it was quite boring.

Father: Really? Didn't you think the players were good? I thought they were awesome.

Liam: I thought they were slow and quite old.

Father: Old? They were younger than me!

2 You will hear a mum describing a new neighbour to her daughter, Jane.

Mum: Hi Jane. How was school today?

Jane: It was awful. How was your day?

Mum: Really nice, thank you. I met our new neighbour.

Jane: Oh, who is it?

Mum: She's a lovely older lady called Maggie.

Jane: Oh no! An old woman. She won't like living next to a noisy teenager. Is she very old-fashioned?

Mum: Don't be awful. No, she's really cool. She wears modern clothes and she's really fun to talk to. She was a teacher.

Jane: Hmmm…

Mum: Don't be so negative, Jane.

3 You will hear a boy, William, talking to his friend, Lucia, about his homework.

Lucia: Hi William. Have you done the geography homework?

William: Hi Lucia. Do you mean the model? Yes, I have but I'm not very satisfied with it.

Lucia: Oh, why not?

William: Well, I was making my model when my dad came home from work. He got all excited about it and wanted to help me make it.

Lucia: That was kind, wasn't it?

William: Hmmm… sort of… but my Dad really isn't very good at making models or geography. He didn't listen to my ideas or let me do any of the work. I tried to be patient, but I just got annoyed with him. Then we had an argument. And my model is terrible.

Lucia: Why don't you change it?

William: I don't think there's enough time.

Unit 7 Sport

Vocabulary

Track 17

1 Listen and tick the correct photo.

1 ice hockey 2 boxing 3 athletics 4 snowboarding
5 water skiing

Track 18

2 Write the sports under the photos in Exercise 1. Then listen and check.

1 A ice hockey B ice skating   2 A boxing B yoga
3 A gymnastics B athletics   4 A skiing B snowboarding
5 A sailing B water skiing

Speaking

Track 19

Some friends are going to the sports centre together. Here are some sports they could do there. Describe each of the sports and say which would/wouldn't be the most fun to do with friends and why.

Listening

Track 20

For each question, choose the correct answer.

1 Which sport did the girl do at school?

Dad: How was tennis? Did you win?
Girl: We didn't play tennis today. The teacher was ill.
Dad: So didn't you do any sports?
Girl: Well, we were going to play football but my friends and I decided to go running instead.

2 What day is the badminton competition?

Billy: Miss, I'm competing in the badminton competition next week. It's on Wednesday, isn't it?
Teacher: It was on Wednesday, but now the drama club need the sports hall, so the badminton competition is on Tuesday.
Billy: Tuesday! But I play squash on a Tuesday. Can the badminton competition be on Monday?
Teacher: Sorry, Billy. No, it can't.

3 Where is Curtis?

Boy: Hello?
Mum: Hi Curtis, it's Mum.
Boy: Oh, hi Mum.
Mum: I'm in the school car park. Where are you? Are you still on the football pitch?
Boy: No, we finished early so I went for a swim afterwards. I'm getting changed now. I'll be five minutes.
Mum: Great. See you then.

Unit 8 Work and jobs

Speaking

Track 21

Listen and answer the questions about work and jobs.

1 Tell me about a job you'd like to do when you're older.
2 Would you like to work as a volunteer? Why or why not?

3 Do you think it's better to go to university or to get a job when you leave school?
4 Do you think teenagers should get part-time work? At what age?
5 What do you think are the advantages and disadvantages of working in an office?

Listening

Track 22

For each question, write the correct answer in the gap. Write one or two words, or a number, or a date, or a time.

You will hear a woman called Vicky Hunter talking about her job.

Hi, I'm Vicky Hunter and I think I've got the best job in the world. I'm a vet – but I don't work with pets, like cats or dogs. I work with elephants. Elephants are awesome animals. I live in India and there are lots of elephants here. Lots of them get sick and I help to make them better. When you work with these animals, you have to be very calm. They're very big and they're also quite nervous. If they're frightened, they might run at you. I'm actually a very loud person so it was quite challenging for me when I first started working with them. But now they're relaxed with me and I can help them. The first time you touch an elephant is amazing. Their skin is quite soft. And I love their big brown eyes.

Unfortunately, I'm leaving my job at the end of December, on the 30th of December actually. I'm very sad about it and I'll really miss India and the elephants. But my sister who lives in Australia is having a baby and I want to go home to see him or her. When I'm in Australia, I'll get another job. I might work as a vet again, maybe in a zoo, but what I'd really like to be one day is a pilot, so I might go back to college!

Unit 9 Entertainment and media

Vocabulary

Track 23

1 Listen and write each word under the correct photo.

ballet, circus, fireworks, orchestra, selfie, audience, headphones, guitarists, journalist

Speaking

Track 24

Here is a photograph. It shows a type of entertainment. Tell me what you can see in the photograph.

Listening

Track 25

For each question, choose the correct answer.

You will hear a radio interview with a young boy who goes to a special school.

Interviewer: Hi Jack. Thanks for coming on our programme today. So, tell us about your school.

Jack: Hi. Well, my school isn't a normal school, it's an entertainment school.

Interviewer: So… for young people who want to become actors and actresses?

Jack: Yes, and for children that are already doing some acting, but also for students who want to be dancers, musicians, circus performers…

Interviewer: Wow!

Jack: Yes, there are lots of very talented people at my school. It's very exciting.

Interviewer: And you went to this school when you were quite young, didn't you?

Jack: Yes. I left my primary school when I was eight to go to my new school because I wanted to be an actor. I wasn't very good at some school subjects like maths or science. I found school quite hard and a bit boring. And I never liked sports very much, or art or crafts, but I did lots of drama and I was in every school play. I don't know if the plays were very good, but I thought they were fun. One day, a teacher from the entertainment school came to see one of my school plays. It was a comedy and I remember that I had to wear long yellow socks and a red jacket and sing a silly song… anyway, after the performance she phoned my parents and said that she thought I was very good at acting. She asked them whether I would like to join her school. She told them to ask me. I remember after the phone call, my parents came into my bedroom and asked me if I liked my school and my friends and if I really liked acting. I said it was fun. They told me about the entertainment school and how most of the classes would be acting, dance or singing and I loved the idea and asked if I could go there.

Interviewer: So you changed schools. And did you like it?

Jack: Yes, I did and I still do. I'm still not very good at the traditional school subjects, but this school has made me feel good at something. I'm 14 and I've already performed in ten plays and I've acted in two TV advertisements. I'm happy to talk to and work with lots of people that I don't know. It's great!

Unit 10 Communication and technology

Vocabulary

Track 26

1 Listen and write each word under the correct photo.

calculator, email, envelope, keyboard, laptop, mouse, parcel, postcard, robot, webcam, text message, photograph

Speaking

Track 27

Listen and answer the questions about technology.

1 Do you have a mobile phone? Is it a smartphone?
2 Could you live without a smartphone? Why or why not?
3 Do you think smartphones should be allowed at school?
4 Do you use technology to help you learn English?
5 How do you use technology to communicate with your friends?

Listening

Track 28

For each question, choose the correct answer.

1 How did the girl finally contact her grandma?

Girl: Hey, Grandma, you got my message!

Grandma: Yes, I did.

Girl: That's great. I tried to phone you on your home phone, but you didn't answer, then I wrote you an email, but it didn't send, so then I thought I'd just send you a text message.

2 What does the dad want for his birthday?

Boy: Hey Dad, what do you want for your birthday?

Dad: Ooh! Well, let me think. I like cameras, but I did get a new one last year so I suppose I don't really need one of those… My laptop's getting a bit old, but a new laptop would be very expensive… I know, I'd really like a new mobile phone because the screen on mine is broken.

3 What isn't broken?

Boy: Mum, Dad, I'm really sorry but I was doing my maths homework on the computer when I spilled some tea on the mouse and it stopped working. I was so angry that I threw my calculator across the room and it broke the TV screen. At least my calculator is fine!

Unit 11 Health, medicine and exercise

Vocabulary

Track 29

1 Listen and tick the correct photo.

1 pills 2 pharmacy 3 headache 4 operation 5 bones

Track 30

2 Write the words under the photos in Exercise 1. Then listen and check.

1 A pills B bandages 2 A gym B pharmacy
3 A earache B headache 4 A operation B accident
5 A bones B brain

Speaking

Track 31

Here is a photograph. It shows a father and son. Tell me what you can see in the photograph.

Listening

Track 32

For each question, write the correct answer in the gap. Write one or two words, or a number, or a date, or a time.

You will hear a girl named Kissy talking about an accident.

Hi I'm Kissy. I'm eleven years old. I'll be twelve in March. I hope my leg will be better by then because I want to go to a water park with swimming pools and slides with my friends.

Two months ago, I was riding my bike on our street when a car came around the corner. The driver was driving too fast. The car hit me. My leg was bleeding and my knee was very painful. I couldn't stand up. My neighbour saw the accident and called my parents. They were very upset. Dad tried to phone for an ambulance but his phone battery wasn't working. So another neighbour phoned for one. I remember the driver of the car was standing next to me, crying. There was a crowd of people in the street and I was embarrassed and very confused. I just wanted to go home. When the ambulance arrived, I already had a really bad headache too. The ambulance took me to hospital. A nurse put a bandage on my leg to stop the bleeding, but she couldn't give me any aspirin because the doctor said I needed to have an operation on my knee.

The operation lasted for three hours. My poor parents were very worried. I stayed in hospital for two days and then I was allowed to go home. I had to stay in bed or on the sofa for three weeks. It was very boring.

Unit 12 Places: Buildings

Speaking

Track 33

Listen and answer the questions about buildings.

1 If you had to show someone around your town or city, which places would you take them to?
2 Tell me about the oldest building in your town.
3 Do you like to shop in department stores? Why or why not?
4 Do you think more teenagers go to bookshops or to libraries? Why?
5 Would you prefer to have a new stadium or a new shopping mall in your town or city? Why?

Listening

Track 34

For each question, choose the correct answer.

1 Where is the woman's car?

Paula: Hi Tony. It's Paula. My car's broken down.
Tony: Oh no! Where are you? Have you taken your car to a garage?
Paula: I'm waiting for a mechanic to come out and fix it. Uh! Can you believe it – I'm at some traffic lights and I'm causing a traffic jam!
Tony: Don't worry. I'll come and get you. I need to go to the bank anyway.

2 Which shop has just opened in town?

Radio presenter: Now, listeners who live in the area might be interested in the latest addition to the town centre. The high street now has its very own bookshop. You'll find it where the hairdresser's used to be, on the corner. Give them your mobile phone number and they'll send you a text about any new books that arrive.

3 Where are the friends going to meet?

Sara: Hi Carol. I'm just calling about our theatre night on Friday. I've spoken to everyone else and we've decided to meet about an hour before the play starts. I've booked the seats, by the way – we're right at the front. And there's a car park at the back of the theatre if you're going to drive. We'll be in the café across the road waiting for you. I'll order you a coffee.

Unit 13 Places: Countryside

Vocabulary

Track 35

1 Listen and write the words in the correct places.

harbour, ocean, bay, cliff, rock, island, hills

Speaking

Track 36

Joy and her family are going on holiday. Here are some places they could go. Describe each of the places and say which would be the most interesting to go to for a holiday.

Listening

Track 37

For each question, choose the correct answer.

You will hear a radio interview with a woman called Kim.

Interviewer:	Hi Kim, welcome to the programme.
Kim:	Thank you. It's lovely to be here.
Interviewer:	So, you run a holiday programme for children who live in the city, don't you?
Kim:	Yes, that's right. I'm very lucky because I live in a beautiful area of the country. I live on a big farm in a valley, surrounded by forest. The nearest village is five miles away. And you have to take a train to get to the city. There's lots of space and lots of things to do. So, I work with city schools to provide holidays for groups of schoolchildren and their teachers on my farm. I think all children should experience the countryside. It's really important.
Interviewer:	So what do the children do when they come?
Kim:	Oh, so many different things! We show them the animals on the farm. Most of the children love the horses. Often these children haven't seen the types of birds we have here and they are amazed by them. We go walking, we climb trees, we do paintings of the scenery and if the weather's hot, we swim in a nearby lake. We don't have a TV here so in the evenings we sit outside, light a fire and cook food on it and look at the stars. We don't allow the children to bring mobile phones or tablets with them either.
Interviewer:	Why not?
Kim:	We really want them to take time to look at what's around them and to listen to the sounds of the countryside. When they do, they often can't believe how noisy the countryside is.
Interviewer:	I'm sure they love these holidays.
Kim:	Yes, most of them do, but of course, there are some children who don't like being outside all the time and they prefer to be in the city. They miss playing video games and going to the shops or to the cinema.

Unit 14 Places: Town and city

Speaking

Track 38

Here is a photograph. It shows a mother and son in a town. Tell me what you can see in the photograph.

Listening

Track 39

For each question, choose the correct answer.

1 You will hear two friends talking about a new monument in their town.

Boy:	Hi Maria, what do you think of the new monument in the town square?
Girl:	Actually, I haven't seen it.
Boy:	Haven't you? It's of William Shakespeare.
Girl:	I wonder why they decided to put up a statue of him. He doesn't come from this town. I think a monument of Mo Farah would be better – he's a sports hero, and he was born in the street next to mine.
Boy:	Oh! I really like it. I think he was an amazing writer and he's really important. And it's a really cool statue. You should see it.

2 You will hear a woman asking a man for directions.

Woman:	Excuse me. Could you tell me the way to Harbour Bridge please?
Man:	Yes, of course. It's quite easy to get there from here.
Woman:	Great! Do I need to go through the park?
Man:	No, you don't. You can go through the town square and cross over the main road.
Woman:	So, I should go through the tunnel?
Man:	No, just go over the bridge. It's safer.
Woman:	Thanks.

3 You will hear a boy, Eddie, telling his friend about a recent trip to a city.

Girl:	Hi Eddie, how was your trip?
Eddie:	It wasn't great.
Girl:	Really? Why not?
Eddie:	Well, the city was really crowded. I hated going on the underground. People were pushing to get on the trains. And we had to go on so many trains to get around because the city is too big to walk around.

Unit 15 Environment

Speaking

Track 40

Some students are discussing the worst things a person can do for the environment. Here are some of their ideas. Discuss these things and say which is the worst.

Listening

Track 41

For each question, choose the correct answer.

You will hear a radio interview with a boy called Chris.

Interviewer: Hi Chris, thanks for joining us today. So you're only ten years old and still at school, and you have done an amazing thing. Can you tell us about it?

Chris: Hi. Well, I read an article in a magazine about how rubbish in the sea is killing sea animals so I organised a big beach clean-up where I live.

Interviewer: Amazing! I've got a photo of the event here. There are lots of people. How many people actually came along?

Chris: About five hundred.

Interviewer: Wow! Were you expecting that many people to come?

Chris: No, I thought maybe thirty or forty would come, mainly my friends and their families, but so many people I didn't know came too.

Interviewer: Why do you think they came?

Chris: Well, I made a podcast about it and I put it online. Apparently lots of people listened to it and then they decided to come and help.

Interviewer: And now you're doing radio and TV interviews about it, aren't you?

Chris: Yes, that's right. I think it's great to be able to talk about it. It's so important. Unless we all do something to help – and we all can – the planet will just get worse and worse. I'm only a child and I'd like there to still be a green and healthy planet when I'm an adult and a parent and later, a grandparent.

Unit 16 Shopping

Vocabulary

Track 42

1 Listen and write each word under the correct photo.

logo, closed, mall, credit cards, supermarket, shop assistant, price, money, customer, label, pay, receipt

Speaking

Track 43

Listen and answer the questions about shopping.

1 How often do you go shopping?
2 What do you like to buy?
3 Tell me about something you have bought recently.
4 Who do you prefer to go shopping with? Why?
5 What do you think are the advantages and disadvantages of shopping online?

Listening

Track 44

For each question, choose the correct answer.

1 How much will the shop assistant sell the chair for?

Woman: I'm interested in that chair – the one for £80, but it's a bit expensive. Can you make it any cheaper?

Man: Oh, it's a luxury chair, madam. I think the price is quite reasonable. However, I could take ten per cent off, and sell it for £72.

Woman: Thank you, but that's still more than I wanted to spend. What about £60?

Man: Oh, I'm afraid that's the cheapest I can sell it for, madam.

2 Which item is the man selling?

Woman: Hi Steve. Where are you going?

Man: To the shop. I want to put this notice in their window.

Woman: Hmmm, sorry. I can't read it. I haven't got my glasses.

Man: (laughing) I'm selling something. We bought a rug the other day but decided we don't really like it. I'm hoping somebody might buy it if I put an advert in the shop window. We sold a sofa that way a few weeks ago so maybe we'll be successful again.

3 How much does the camera in the shop cost?

Woman: Could I have a look at that camera please?

Shop assistant: Here you are, madam. It's a great little camera.

Woman: I've seen it advertised online for £80. How much are you selling it for?

Shop assistant: Hmmm, £80 seems very cheap to me. We're currently selling it for £95 – it's reduced from £125 for one month.

Unit 17 Weather

Speaking

Track 45

Here is a photograph. It shows a woman going home. Tell me what you can see in the photograph.

Listening

Track 46

For each question, choose the correct answer.

1 You will hear two friends talking about a hike they went on last Saturday.

Man: Do you want to go for another hike this weekend? The weather forecast says it will be sunny and cool.

Woman: I'm not sure. The weather forecast for last Saturday was completely wrong. It said it was going to be mild and sunny with a few short showers, but there was a storm and we got really wet on that hike.

2 You will hear a mother and son talking about the weather.

Boy: Mum, why didn't you wake me up? I'm going to be late for school.

Mum: Sorry, Harry, but you can't go to school this morning.

Boy: Oh? Why not?

Mum: The weather's too bad.

Boy: Is it snowing? Do you remember last year when it snowed? The school was closed!

Mum: Oh yes, you stayed home for three days. But this time it's because of the gale. The headteacher is worried that the big trees might fall onto the school building. Don't worry though, it's supposed to stop this afternoon and then it's just going to be cold and cloudy.

3 You will hear a man and woman planning a holiday.

Man: So, where shall we go on holiday this year?

Woman: If we're going in the summer, then I'd like to go somewhere hot and sunny, so that we can swim in the sea and sunbathe.

Man: That sounds fantastic, but I don't think I can go in the summer. We could go in the winter though.

Woman: OK, but in the winter I don't really like going to hot places.

Man: Do you prefer to go to places with snow?

Woman: No. I don't like snow or ice. I actually prefer places that are wet and foggy and really cold. I love walking in the countryside and getting really wet and cold and coming back to a nice hotel and getting warm and having a nice meal.

Unit 18 Travel and transport

Vocabulary

Track 47

1 Listen and tick the correct photo.

1 astronaut 2 brochures 3 rocket 4 handlebars
5 parking space

Track 48

2 Write the words under the photos in Exercise 1. Then listen and check.

1 A astronaut B backpacker 2 A brochures
B guidebooks 3 A ferry B rocket 4 A handlebars
B mirror 5 A parking space B waiting room

Speaking

Track 49

Some students are discussing ways to travel around town. Here are some of their ideas. Discuss these things and say which is the best.

Listening

Track 50

For each question, write the correct answer in the gap. Write one or two words, or a number, or a date, or a time.

You will hear a boy named Charlie talking about a journey.

Hi I'm Charlie. I'm thirteen years old and I've just been to Scotland and I wanted to tell you about the fantastic journey. We went on the train, it's called The Caledonian Sleeper. It's called a sleeper train because you sleep on it. The journey took thirteen hours. We got on at Euston station in London at 9.15 pm and arrived in Fort William in Scotland at 10.15 am the next day. My room was amazing. It had a double bed and a little bathroom. There was a restaurant on the train and we had a lovely dinner before bed. I had Scottish salmon and potatoes, and I had some lovely ice cream for dessert. I slept really well as the bed was very comfortable.

My whole family enjoyed the experience and we've already booked another sleeper train journey that goes from London to Cornwall, in the south-west of England.

Unit 19 The natural world

Speaking

Track 51

Listen and answer the questions about the natural world.

1 What wildlife is there where you live?
2 What is your favourite season and why?
3 What is the countryside like where you live?
4 Have you ever been to the coast or to the mountains? Can you describe what it was like to me?
5 Do you think it's important to look after the natural world? Why or why not?

Listening

Track 52

For each question, choose the correct answer.

1 You will hear two friends talking about an island.

Boy: Did you hear about Dunstall Island?

Girl: I did read something about the island – something to do with water, I think. Was it a bad flood after the storm? I think I read about a big wave that came from the sea.

Boy: No, it wasn't actually. There was a bad fire because it was so hot and dry.

2 You will hear two friends talking online.

Woman: Hi Mark, how are you?

Man: I'm good thanks, Natalie. But it's raining here today.

Woman: Oh no! I suppose it rains a lot in winter where you are.

Man: Yes, it does, but it's not really winter here yet. It's still autumn. It's usually quite nice and sunny in the autumn – but not today. What's it like with you?

Woman: (laughing) It's hot and sunny here because it's the middle of summer.

Man: I'm jealous!

3 You will hear a tour guide talking about some of the animals in her country.

Woman: Welcome to Australia. It's a beautiful country but you should take care; some animals can hurt you. Now, I know lots of people are scared of sharks and we do get sharks in the ocean in some areas. But these attacks are rare.
Secondly, do please use a cream to stop 'mossies' from biting you. That's what we call mosquitos here. Their bites are no fun. If you are bitten, just go to the pharmacy and get some cream.
Finally, in the countryside, you will see lots of kangaroos. You can take photos but don't try to go near them. Kangaroos are big animals, and they can kick. If one kicks you, it may break your arm or leg. Lots of people get hurt by kangaroos every year – many more than those who get hurt by sharks.

Unit 20 Language

Speaking
Track 53

Some students are discussing the best ways to practise a language.

Here are some of their ideas. Discuss these things and say which is best.

Listening
Track 54

For each question, choose the correct answer.

You will hear a podcast with a girl called Ruby.

Interviewer: Hi Ruby, thanks for being here today. Ruby you speak six different languages. How have you learned so many?

Ruby: Hi. Well, my mum is Spanish and my dad is English so I've grown up hearing two different languages at home and I think that has really helped.

Interviewer: But you also speak Chinese, French, German and Turkish. Are those languages you heard at home too?

Ruby: No, not at all. My parents don't speak any other languages. I went to an international school so I heard a lot of other languages there as well. At school I had to communicate with people from lots of different countries with lots of different first languages. We spoke English in our lessons but at break times and when we hung out together outside of school, my friends would speak their own languages too. I think hearing all those different sounds every day really helped to develop my listening skills. I find listening to foreign languages really easy.

Interviewer: And has that helped with your speaking?

Ruby: Definitely. Because I can hear the different sounds in a language quite clearly, I don't find it too difficult to pronounce the words. But sometimes I get it wrong and then my friends laugh at me – but I keep trying.

Interviewer: And did you learn each language you speak just by chatting to your friends?

Ruby: No, not completely – I had to learn the grammar and lots of vocabulary too. I think it's important to be able to read in a language you speak so that if you go to that country, you will be able to understand signs and notices and all those kinds of things. That's quite hard, because in some languages – and English is one of these – the words aren't always written as they sound. But I'm not afraid of working hard to learn a language – I love languages.

Interviewer: So how did you learn to read in these languages?

Ruby: Well, I actually read books in foreign languages with the translations. I like to compare both. I find that helps me to understand the grammar better.

Interviewer: Finally, do you have any advice on how to learn another language?

Ruby: Ummm... I think my best advice is don't worry about making mistakes, listen to the language and have a go at speaking it as often as possible and definitely ask for help when you need it.

Unit 1 Clothes and accessories

Vocabulary

1 1 dress 2 bracelet 3 socks 4 handbag
5 raincoat 6 ring 7 necklace 8 backpack
9 glasses 10 perfume 11 earring
12 tracksuit

2 1 laundry 2 pocket 3 uniform 4 label
5 underwear 6 material 7 make-up 8 kit
9 size 10 pattern

3 1 woollen 2 cotton 3 silk 4 plastic

Grammar Box

Sample answers:

1 I'm wearing a pink jumper and black jeans.
I'm not wearing any socks or shoes.

2 I'm practising for the Cambridge Preliminary
exam.

3 They're doing the washing up.

Speaking

Suggested answers:

1 I really like casual clothes, like tracksuits and
trainers, anything that's really comfortable,
like big jumpers or big T-shirts. I don't like
tight jeans or shoes – clothes you can't
move in.

2 I don't buy new clothes very often.
Sometimes I go shopping in town with my
mum or dad, but usually I get clothes as
presents for my birthday.

3 Yes, I do. It's dark green. We have to wear
a dress and tights or a shirt and tie with a
jacket and trousers. I hate it!

4 I don't mind wearing the same clothes as
my friends. Sometimes, I wear my best
friend's clothes and she wears mine, which
is nice. We like the same clothes.

5 I don't wear a watch but I always wear
earrings. I carry my backpack to school
every day.

Reading

1 D **2** F **3** G **4** B **5** A

Listening

1 16 **2** 21 **3** jeans **4** belts

Writing

Sample answer:

Dear Miss White,

In my opinion, we should change the colour
of the school uniform. I don't like brown and
I would prefer black because I think that black
is very smart. I wouldn't like girls to wear skirts.
I think both boys and girls should wear black
trousers, white shirts and black jackets. In the
winter, we could also have a jumper. This could
be in a different colour, for example red. I think
we should be allowed to wear trainers that are
black as I wouldn't like to have to wear shoes.
Trainers are more comfortable.

I think students should be allowed to wear
small earrings, one or two rings and a necklace
if they want to.

Kim

Grammar Box

Sample answer: I'm going to the gym with my
brother.

Unit 2 Education

Vocabulary

1 1 B 2 A 3 A 4 A 5 B

2 1 A ruler   B rubber
2 A library   B classroom
3 A pupil   B teacher
4 A pencil case   B dictionary
5 A music lesson   B art lesson

3 1 exams 2 qualifications 3 university
4 degree 5 project 6 research 7 notes
8 remember 9 course 10 college 11 level
12 primary 13 clever 14 lessons

Speaking

Sample answer:

In this photo there are five secondary school
students. They are sitting at desks. They are
wearing black and white school uniforms.
I think they are doing a test because the desks

are in a line and they are not talking to each other. There is some paper, and pens and pencils on each desk. The girl at the front of the photo looks worried, so I think the test is difficult for her. The boy behind her is writing, so maybe it's easier for him.

Reading

1 E 2 A 3 D 4 B

Grammar Box

Sample answers:

1 If it rains tomorrow, I'll go to school by bus.
2 If Mum or Dad asks me to tidy my room, I'll say OK.

Listening

1 A 2 C

Writing

Sample answer:

Dear Ms Finch,

I'm very excited about meeting the exchange students from the UK next month.

I think a school trip is a great idea. Why don't we take them to the art museum? It's a lovely building and the paintings are beautiful. There's a special exhibition of photography at the moment.

I would prefer to make a video rather than do a play in English because I feel nervous when I speak English in front of people.

I'm sorry, but I won't be able to meet the exchange students when they arrive as I am playing in a football match that day.

Thanks,

Nick

Unit 3 Food and drink

Vocabulary

1 Across: 2 peach 3 herbs 5 coconut
   7 melon 9 peanut 11 broccoli
   Down: 1 beans 4 salmon 5 cabbage
   6 cucumber 8 flour 9 pie 10 toast 12 onion
2 1 slice 2 ingredients 3 snack 4 taste 5 sour
   6 vegetarian 7 microwave 8 spicy 9 sweet
   10 refreshments 11 recipe 12 pan

Speaking

Suggested answers:

1 In this picture there are two children enjoying a picnic in the park. I think that they are having a good time.
2 In this picture there are two children having a pizza together. They have nearly finished their meals and they look happy.
3 In this picture there is a group of people at a party. They are having a barbecue. It's really sunny. It looks fun.
4 In the last picture there are two girls, maybe friends, having a snack together. I think they're eating burgers.

In my opinion, the barbecue looks fun because it is so sunny, and they're having a good time.

Reading

1 A 2 B 3 D 4 B 5 A 6 A

Grammar Box

Sample answer:

To make a fruit salad, **first** cut some strawberries. **Then** peel a banana. **Next** peel and cut an orange. Mix the fruits together in a bowl and **after that** add some orange juice. **Finally**, divide the fruit salad into bowls and eat with cream.

Listening

1 A 2 C 3 C

Writing

Sample answer:

I wanted this to be the best meal Sarah had ever eaten. I knew Sarah loved cheese, so first I looked for recipes with cheese in all my parents' cookbooks. But the recipes were very complicated. Next, I looked for recipes online, but the best recipes needed many different ingredients. I wasn't sure what to do, so I decided to go to the supermarket. I bought lots of different cheeses. When I got home, I looked at all the cheeses. What could I do with them? It was 6.30 and Sarah was coming to my house at 7.00. I phoned my sister and asked for her help. She told me to cut the cheeses into pieces, bake them in the oven with herbs and chilli and slice some bread to eat it with. Sarah loved it!

Unit 4 Hobbies and leisure

Vocabulary

1 1 sunbathing 2 playing guitar 3 hiking
4 ice skating 5 playing chess 6 at a festival
7 at a gallery 8 on a cruise 9 sightseeing
10 sculpture 11 jogging 12 at a party

2 1 going out 2 hang out 3 keen on 4 went
shopping 5 joining in

3 1 campsite 2 ice skates 3 sightseeing
4 opening hours 5 playground

Speaking

Suggested answers:

1 I like going out with my friends to the city
centre.

2 I think children my age are often keen on
ice skating and sports.

3 I've never played a musical instrument.
I'd like to learn how to play one.

4 I like hanging out with my friends in the
park because we can play games together.
Everyone can join in.

5 The advantages of being a member of a
club are that you can get better at a sport
and play in a team. A disadvantage of being
a member of a club is that it is sometimes
expensive.

Reading

1 D 2 C 3 A

Listening

1 countryside 2 writing stories 3 six
4 Honey Cake 5 drawing

Grammar Box

Sample answers:

1 If I met someone famous, I would ask for a
selfie with them.

2 If I found a puppy in my street, I wouldn't
keep it. I would try to find the owner.

Writing

Sample answer:

Dear Mr Hammond,

Thank you for your email and for letting me
know about the ice-skating club sessions this
term. I'm very excited!

I don't think I can come to the first session as
I have dance club until 5.15, but I'd like to
come to the second and third sessions please.

Yes, I'd like to take an ice-skating exam this
year. When will the exams be? What level
could I do?

Perhaps we could encourage more people to
join the club if we did an ice-skating show for
people to watch.

Thanks

Maisie

Unit 5 House and home

Vocabulary

1 1 ceiling 2 microwave 3 fridge 4 cupboard
5 bulb 6 mug 7 bowl 8 sink 9 drawer
10 oven

2 1 cellar 2 antique 3 handle 4 lock 5 blind
6 rent 7 neighbour 8 flatmate

3 1 A 2 C 3 D 4 A 5 D 6 B 7 C 8 B 9 A
10 B 11 A 12 D

Speaking

Suggested answers:

1 I live in Bristol, in the UK.

2 I live with my mum, my dad and my
younger brother.

3 I live in a flat in the centre of the city.

Reading

1 B 2 C 3 B

Grammar Box

1 which 2 who 3 that 4 whose

Listening

1 C 2 B 3 B 4 C

Writing

Sample answer:

It was dark as I walked up the path to the front
door, which was open! I shouted 'hello' but
nobody answered. I pushed open the door.
There were no lights on in the hall. I tried the
light switch, but the lights didn't go on. I took
out my phone and turned on the torch. The
house was cold. I wondered where everyone was.

I was scared. Then I heard a noise coming from the dining room. I walked slowly towards the door. I carefully opened the door. 'Surprise!' The lights came on. All my family and friends were there. It was a party for me!

Unit 6 Personal feelings, opinions and experiences

Vocabulary

1 1 jealous 2 miserable 3 patient 4 generous
5 cute 6 ashamed 7 anxious 8 bossy
9 delighted

Grammar Box

1 annoying **2** annoyed

2 1 amazing 2 excited 3 interested
4 frightening 5 confusing 6 boring
7 embarrassed 8 disappointed

3 1 reliable 2 cheerful 3 challenging 4 gentle
5 cruel 6 rude 7 unusual

Speaking

Sample answer:

In this photograph there's a man and his son. They're outside by a river or a lake. There are lots of trees by the water. It's a sunny day. I think it's hot because the boy is wearing shorts and a shirt. His dad is wearing jeans, a T-shirt and a shirt. They're fishing together and the boy has just caught a fish. The dad is putting the fish in a silver bucket. They're both smiling and look really happy. The boy looks proud that he has caught the fish.

Reading

1 but **2** could **3** soon **4** 'll/will **5** not **6** when

Grammar Box

1 was eating; went **2** was running; bit

Listening

1 B **2** B **3** C

Writing

Sample answer:

I was reading a book in the garden when I heard a strange noise. It was coming from my neighbour's garden. I looked over the fence. In the middle of the garden, there was a big white bird. It had hurt its wing. I climbed over the fence and walked over to the bird, but it wasn't very friendly and it tried to bite me. I didn't like this bird so I went back to my house and I put some loud music on.

An hour later, the bird had gone. I felt a bit guilty that I hadn't helped it, so I didn't tell anyone about it.

Unit 7 Sport

Vocabulary

1 1 A 2 A 3 B 4 B 5 B

2 1A ice hockey 1B ice skating 2A boxing
2B yoga 3A gymnastics 3B athletics
4A skiing 4B snowboarding 5A sailing
5B water skiing

3 1 athlete 2 competitor 3 goalkeeper
4 cyclist 5 champion 6 rider 7 changing
room 8 pitch 9 stadium 10 court

4 1 T 2 F – People drive cars around a race
track. 3 T 4 F – This is an extreme sport.

Grammar Box

Sample answer: In football, tracksuits must be worn to training sessions.

Speaking

Sample answer:

The pictures show table tennis, climbing, a baseball game and skateboarding. I really like skateboarding and I often go to the park with my friends, so I think this would be a fun activity to do in a group. I think that the problem with table tennis is that you usually play with two or four people, so if there are more than four people in the group someone has to watch. That wouldn't be a lot of fun. I think climbing is a nice sport, but again, it's not great for groups. It's better when you are alone. I suppose if there are lots of people and it's sunny, then baseball would be a great game to play with your friends, but I prefer skateboarding.

Reading

1 C **2** A **3** D

Listening

1 B **2** B **3** B

Writing

Sample answer:

I'm 13 years old and I love doing sport. I'm a member of the football, rugby and ice hockey teams at school. I also go sailing with my mum at weekends. Most of my friends enjoy doing sports too. I think it's really important for teenagers to do sports because we work very hard in our subjects at school and we need to relax. If you are a member of a sports club or team, you can make new friends too. It's also good to be healthy and not sit and watch TV or play computer games every evening and weekend.

Unit 8 Work and jobs

Vocabulary

1 Across: 3 librarian 4 nurse 6 unemployed
8 babysitter 9 chef 11 lecturer
12 journalist
Down: 1 volunteer 2 crew 4 novelist
5 guard 7 detective 8 butcher 10 soldier
12 judge

2 1 retiring 2 tour guide 3 part-time
4 volunteer 5 salary

Grammar Box

Sample answer:

1 This weekend I'm visiting my grandparents.

2 I'm taking my Preliminary English exam in February.

Speaking

Suggested answers:

1 When I'm older I'd like to be an architect. I think it would be fun to draw and design buildings such as schools and hotels.

2 Yes, I would like to work as a volunteer. I think you would meet lots of interesting people and do some good things that help your community.

3 I think it's better to get a job when you leave school, because if you go to university you don't have any money.

4 Yes, I think teenagers should get part-time jobs because they want money to go shopping and to go out with their friends. But I don't think they should work too much or they won't be able to study. I think a good age to get a part-time job is about 15.

5 I think an advantage of working in an office is that you have your own desk and computer. In most offices you work with the same people every day so you can make good friends. I think a disadvantage is that you are inside all day and I like being outside when it's sunny weather.

Reading

1 E **2** B **3** D **4** C

Grammar Box

Sample answer:

1 This year school closes on 25th June for the summer holidays.

2 I have English class next on Tuesday at 2 p.m.

Listening

1 vet **2** elephants **3** India **4** calm
5 30th December **6** pilot

Writing

Sample answer:

Dear Ollie,

Thanks for your email. That's great that you can cut my hair.

I'd prefer to come on Monday next week because I'm going to the theatre on Friday with my English class.

I can't come in the morning because I'm at school. What about 4.30 p.m.? I leave school at 3.30 and I will get the bus into town.

I've got quite long dark brown hair and I would like it to be much shorter.

I'm looking forward to meeting you too.

Thanks,

Jo

Unit 9 Entertainment and media

Vocabulary

1 1 fireworks 2 headphones 3 audience 4 journalist 5 orchestra 6 selfie 7 circus 8 guitarists 9 ballet

2 1 interval 2 interviewer 3 series 4 scene; hero 5 podcasts

3 1 C 2 B 3 C 4 A 5 A 6 B 7 C 8 B 9 C 10 A 11 A 12 A

Speaking

Sample answer:

This photo shows a big garden in the evening. In the background there are lots of trees and there is grass on the ground. On the right of the photo is a big tree. Someone has made a cinema in the garden. In the centre of the photo, there is a small screen for a film with lights around it. The screen is made from a bed sheet tied onto some wood. In front of the screen there are three rows of old wooden chairs for the audience, but there aren't any people in this photo. There are nine chairs. There are some snacks on some of the chairs.

Reading

1 A **2** C **3** B

Listening

1 A **2** B **3** C **4** B

Grammar Box

Sample answers:

1 My English teacher said that my homework was excellent.

2 My mum asked me if I would like sausages for dinner.

Writing

Sample answer:

I recommend watching *The Crown*. There are four series to watch.

It's historical because it's the story of the British queen and her family. It's not a soap opera but it feels a bit like one because it's all about their lives. The actors and actresses are wonderful.

The series is filmed in lots of palaces and castles in London and Scotland, so it's very beautiful to look at. It's quite a serious programme, so don't watch it when you want to laugh. I think it's really interesting and it's great if you want to learn a lot about Britain and its history.

Unit 10 Communication and technology

Vocabulary

1 1 calculator 2 laptop 3 parcel 4 envelope 5 robot 6 text message 7 photograph 8 email 9 webcam 10 mouse 11 keyboard 12 postcard

2 1 data 2 password 3 volume 4 podcast 5 chat room 6 upload 7 blogger 8 homepage 9 invention 10 ring

3 1 blogger 2 blogs 3 video clips 4 download 5 app 6 photos 7 delete

Speaking

Suggested answers:

1 Yes, I do have a mobile phone but it isn't a smartphone.

2 No, I couldn't because I use my phone to keep in contact with my friends and to make arrangements to meet.

3 Yes, I do because it's useful to take photos of the board on your phone in class so you can look at it again later when you are doing your homework.

4 No, not really. Though some of my friends watch English programmes online.

5 I use my phone a lot to communicate with my friends on social media. I don't really send emails though.

Reading

1 B **2** D **3** C **4** A **5** A

Grammar Box

Sample answers:

Yes, I had heard about 3D printing before I read this text. / No, I hadn't heard about 3D printing before I read this text.

Listening

1 B 2 B 3 B

Writing

Sample answer:

I couldn't live without my video game headset because I love playing video games online with my friends. I use my headset everyday after school and at the weekends. It's great because I can talk to my friends online and play the same game as them. If I didn't have my headset, I could still play video games, but I wouldn't be able to talk to my friends while I was playing. So it wouldn't be as much fun. I don't really go to my friend's house or to the park with them, so this is how I spend time with them.

Unit 11 Health, medicine and exercise

Vocabulary

1 1 A 2 B 3 B 4 A 5 A
2 1 A pills B bandages
   2 A gym B pharmacy
   3 A earache B headache
   4 A operation B accident
   5 A bones B brain
3 1 hand 2 finger 3 knee 4 toes 5 foot
   6 ankle 7 heel 8 leg
4 1 painful 2 prescription 3 diet 4 sick
   5 patients 6 emergency

Speaking

Sample answer:

In the photo there is a father and his son. They're taking exercise in the park. I think it's autumn because the trees in the background have yellow and orange leaves and there are leaves on the pavement. It isn't a sunny day. The boy and his dad are sitting on the pavement. They both look fit and healthy. They're both wearing tracksuits and trainers. The father is wearing blue tracksuits trousers, a blue T-shirt and white trainers. He's sitting on the left. The boy is on the right. He's wearing blue tracksuit trousers too, a grey top and white and red trainers. I think he is about ten years old. They are sitting on the ground and they have their hands on their heads. They are doing exercises. The dad looks happy but the boy doesn't. He looks unhappy. Maybe his stomach hurts.

Reading

1 F 2 A 3 C 4 H 5 B

Grammar Box

Suggested answers:

1 No, I've never had a tooth taken out.
2 No, I'm not having my hair cut until next week.
3 The last time I had my photo taken was at school in December.

Listening

1 11/eleven 2 2/two 3 neighbour
4 bad headache/headache 5 aspirin
6 2/two days

Writing

Sample answer:

Dear Ms Whittard,

I think it's a great idea to make our school a healthier place.

It would be fantastic to take some exercise together every day. I would prefer to do this before school as I go horse riding most afternoons after school, and I have lots of homework to do too.

I think it would be good to go jogging. It's a good way to keep fit. We could also do some yoga in the hall when it is raining.

A healthy meal I would like to have for lunch at school is chicken salad.

Thanks!
Ali

Unit 12 Places: Buildings

Vocabulary

1 Across: 2 office 4 guest house 5 palace
   7 entrance 11 lift 12 factory
   Down: 1 tower 3 ruin 4 gallery 5 prison
   6 university 8 exit 9 stadium 10 café

Grammar Box

1 are **2** taught

Sample answer:

A bookshop is a place where books are sold.

2 1 F 2 B 3 E 4 J 5 D 6 H 7 G 8 I 9 A 10 C

Speaking

Suggested answers:

1 If I had to show someone around my town, I think I would take them to the art gallery because it has some very famous paintings by Van Gogh in it and it's a beautiful modern building. Then I would take them to the palace. It's very old and very beautiful.

2 The oldest building in my town is a ruin. It was a castle.

3 No, I don't because they are too big and you have to go up and down in the lifts to find the different things you want to buy. I prefer to shop in small shops or online.

4 I don't think many teenagers go to libraries. I'm not sure that they go to bookshops either. I think they buy books online and read them on their phones or tablets.

5 I'd prefer to have a new stadium because I love doing and watching sport.

Reading

1 not **2** by **3** from **4** there **5** if

Grammar Box

1 was **2** built

Sample answer:

A secondary school was built in my town last year.

Listening

1 C **2** B **3** C

Writing

Sample answer:

I'm very proud of the place where I live. My town is very beautiful and historic. It has lots of very interesting buildings, such as the castle, which was built about 700 years ago. It's a ruin now, but it is still my favourite place in the town. There is also an amazing cinema that is very old-fashioned. And in the centre of town there are several rows of houses which are very old too. They're very pretty. I think a new railway station would improve my town because then lots more people could come and visit.

Unit 13 Places: Countryside

Vocabulary

1 1 island 2 cliff 3 harbour 4 hills 5 ocean 6 rock 7 bay

2 1 F 2 F 3 T 4 F 5 T 6 F 7 T 8 F

3 1 earth 2 stream 3 canal 4 port 5 valley 6 scenery 7 region 8 land

Speaking

Sample answer:

So, there's a campsite in the countryside, it's next to a pretty stream. It looks quite peaceful and relaxing. It's surrounded by hills so you could go hiking and have picnics. Then there's a desert with camels in it. It looks hot and sunny there. I think the sand is beautiful. This one is a canal with a very pretty boat on it. The boat is travelling past some fields with animals in them in the countryside. In my opinion it might be a bit boring to go on the boat on the canal. The boat is going quite slowly and the scenery is not that exciting. And this one shows a seaside village with a small beach. It looks like a nice place for a holiday because there is a beach, so you could go swimming, and there are boats so you could go out on a boat in the sea. I really like the seaside, but I think the desert would be the most interesting because it's so unusual – it would be a holiday that you would always remember. What do you think?

Reading

1 A **2** C **3** B **4** D **5** B **6** A

Grammar Box

Sample answer:

In my country it's very hot and dry during the summer, but in September it rains a lot.

Listening

1 C **2** C **3** A **4** B

Writing

Sample answer:

The boat moved slowly up and down on the sea. It was calm now after the storm, but I could see that the sail on the boat was broken. I was in the middle of the ocean, I couldn't see any land and my mobile phone wasn't working. I was worried. I lay on my back and looked up at the sky. It was a pale blue and the sun was behind a cloud. I realised that my clothes were wet from the storm. I felt cold and miserable. I fell asleep. Bang! I woke up. I couldn't believe my eyes. I had landed on a beach. There were lots of people sunbathing on the sand in front of a gorgeous hotel. A waiter came over to me and asked, 'Would you like a drink, sir?'

Unit 14 Places: Town and city

Vocabulary

1　1 cash machine　2 bus stop　3 crossroads
4 fountain　5 monument　6 pavement
7 signpost　8 subway　9 tunnel
10 roundabout　11 petrol station　12 bridge

2　1 route　2 bridge　3 fountain　4 crossing
5 corner

3　1 park　2 playground　3 airport　4 zoo
5 underground 6 square

Grammar Box

1　Can you tell me where Pritti lives?

2　Could you tell me what time the booking office opens?

Speaking

Sample answer:

In this photo I can see a mother and her son at a food market on a sunny day. They're buying vegetables. They are standing next to a vegetable stall. You can see peas, carrots, onions and lots of other nice-looking vegetables in different colours. The mother and son are in the foreground and behind them there are other market stalls and customers. I can see an older couple in the background on the left. The mother is quite young. She's got long brown hair and she's wearing a grey dress and sunglasses. She's looking down at her son,

who I think is about six years old. He's wearing a blue and white top. He's also wearing sunglasses. The mother is holding a bag of vegetables that they have just bought. I think the boy wants to look at it. Maybe he wants to eat something that's inside.

Reading

1 are　**2** 've/have　**3** to　**4** going　**5** where
6 If

Listening

1 A　**2** B　**3** C

Grammar Box

1　I don't know where my phone is.

2　I wonder which way it is to the city centre.

Writing

Sample answer:

Dear Dan,

It's great that you are visiting next week. I can't wait to see you too.

To get to my house from the airport you should take the number 44 bus. The bus stop is outside the airport building. Ask the driver to stop outside the cash machines on Market Street. I'll meet you there.

Yes, of course I'll show you the town on Saturday. We should go to the town square, it's got lots of old buildings and a cool fountain. There are lots of nice cafés there too.

Maybe you could bring my parents a souvenir from your country or some chocolates.

See you soon!

Fred

Unit 15: Environment

Vocabulary

1　Across: 4 climate change　5 volunteer
6 pollution　8 plastic
Down: 1 litter　2 petrol　3 recycle
6 prohibited　7 traffic

2　1 A　2 C

3　1 recycling
2 glass/cans/cardboard
3 glass/cans/cardboard

4 glass/cans/cardboard
5 bottle bank
6 bin

Speaking

Sample answer:

OK, so there is a photo of a shower with the water on. I think this shows that we shouldn't waste water and we should make sure taps are turned off properly after we have used them. This is very important, especially in hot countries that don't have much water. Then there is a photo of a plane. Planes cause a lot of pollution which is very bad for climate change, so people should fly less. I think it's probably worse to fly than to leave a tap on. The next two photos show rubbish. In one someone is throwing a plastic bottle out of the window of their car, and in the other photo someone has left rubbish on the beach. I think it's very bad to not recycle plastic bottles and it's lazy to not put your rubbish in a bin. It makes me very angry. I think it's worse to leave rubbish on a beach than in the countryside because although it doesn't look nice in the countryside, if rubbish gets into the sea it can hurt sea animals. In the last photo, people are cutting down trees. I think it's in a rainforest. I think this is the worst thing you can do for the environment because trees give us clean air. What do you think?

Reading

1 F 2 E 3 D 4 C

Listening

1 C 2 B 3 B 4 B

Grammar Box

Sample answer:

Unless more people use public transport, climate change will get worse.

Writing

Sample answer:

I think the biggest problem the planet has is climate change. Climate change comes from all the pollution in the air and in the sky. It is worse in cities and crowded places where there are often factories and where people use their cars all the time and go on aeroplanes.

Unless people start using public transport more, the problem will continue. So all cities and towns should have good public transport systems. In addition, people should use electric cars rather than petrol cars. But the best type of transport is to walk or to cycle.

Unit 16: Shopping

Vocabulary

1 1 credit cards 2 label 3 mall 4 supermarket
5 receipt 6 shop assistant 7 closed 8 price
9 pay 10 money 11 customer 12 logo

2 1 spend 2 reserve 3 second-hand
4 bargain 5 try on; return 6 shopping
7 ordered 8 expensive 9 damaged;
exchange 10 reduced

Speaking

Suggested answers:

1 I don't go shopping very often. Maybe about once a month.

2 I like buying bags and hats. I don't like buying shoes or going to the supermarket to buy food.

3 Last month I bought a new coat for the winter. It's red and it's got a hood. It wasn't very expensive but it's really nice and warm.

4 I prefer to go shopping with my parents because they buy me lots of nice things.

5 I think an advantage of shopping online is that it is easier than going to the shops, but a disadvantage is that you can't see all the clothes very well, so sometimes it's a bit boring. It's OK if you know what you want to buy – you can do that quite quickly and you can find the cheapest place to buy it, but I like going to shops, especially the mall, just to look around.

Reading

1 D 2 B 3 A 4 A 5 C

Grammar Box

Sample answer:

Yesterday, I went shopping with my sister, Emma. She wanted to buy **some** jeans. We went to the nearest clothes shop but there weren't **any** jeans that she liked, so we got on a bus and went to the mall. There were **lots of** people in the mall and we had to wait to get into **some** shops. I didn't like it, so I went to a café and had a drink. Emma tried on so many jeans, but she didn't buy **any**.

Listening

1 B 2 C 3 B

Writing

Sample answer:

I love shopping. I go to the shops as often as I can. I usually go every weekend. It's really important to me that I have the newest clothes. I see things other people are wearing at school, or in magazines or online and I need to have them. And I love a bargain. I sometimes ask the shop assistants if they can make the price cheaper for me and sometimes they do. I really couldn't live without shopping. I'm very lucky because I have a big shopping mall near to where I live.

Unit 17 Weather

Vocabulary

1   1 lightning 2 sunshine 3 gale 4 icy
    5 forecast 6 temperature
2   1 humid 2 frozen 3 mild 4 dry 5 breeze
    6 shower 7 cool 8 storm 9 wet
    10 thunder
3   1 temperature 2 snowfall 3 heat
    4 weather 5 thunderstorm 6 clouds
    7 ice 8 wet

Speaking

Sample answer:

In this photo, there's a woman standing on an empty railway platform. There isn't anyone else on the platform and there aren't any trains. It's evening and it's snowing. The woman is wearing big brown boots, white trousers, a big green winter coat with the hood up and a big white scarf. It looks very cold. I think it's been snowing for a while as there is quite a lot of snow on the platform. The woman is talking on her mobile phone.

Reading

1 to 2 which 3 well 4 If 5 so 6 them

Grammar Box

Suggested answers:

1   Yes, I have to look after my pet rabbit. I have to give it fresh food and water and clean its cage.
2   No, I don't need to do any homework after school today.
3   When I get to the school in the mornings I must go straight to my classroom.

Listening

1 C 2 B 3 A

Writing

Sample answer:

As soon as Tim's plane landed, he realised he had brought the wrong clothes. He had checked the weather forecast and it had said hot and humid weather, but it was really cold and rainy. Tim had only packed shorts and T-shirts and he wished he had a jumper. In the airport shop the clothes were all too expensive. Tim had no choice. He took all his T-shirts and shorts out of his suitcase and put them all on. Then he walked out of the airport to the taxis, trying to ignore all of the people who were laughing at him.

Unit 18 Travel and transport

Vocabulary

1   1 A 2 A 3 B 4 A 5 A
2   1 A astronaut 1 B backpacker
    2 A brochures 2 B guide books 3 A ferry
    3 B rocket 4 A handlebars 4 B mirror
    5 A parking space 5 B waiting room
3   by: air, land, rail, road, sea
    on: board, business, foot, holiday, time

Speaking

Sample answer:

These photos all show different ways to travel around town. **I agree** buses are a good form of transport because they are better for the environment than cars; they are reliable and they go all around town. That's true. **However,** you do have to pay for them and if you are going on a long journey it can take quite a long time to get there, or you may have to go on more than one bus. Going by car is quicker – **that's a good point**, but it's not great for the environment and it can cause traffic jams. Taxis are also quicker than buses, but they are more expensive and can also cause traffic jams. Walking and cycling are both very good for the environment but if the weather is bad, you get wet. If you are going a long way it can take quite a long time, but both walking and cycling can keep you fit and healthy. So I think either cycling or walking are the best ways to travel around town.

Reading

1 G **2** B **3** A **4** F **5** D

Grammar Box

Sample answer:

I've just eaten my lunch.

Listening

1 13 **2** Scotland **3** train **4** 13 **5** 10.15 a.m. **6** Scottish salmon

Grammar Box

Sample answer:

My friend wants to see the new James Bond film, but I've already seen it.

Writing

Sample answer:

A journey I remember is when I travelled by sea plane to an island in the Maldives. Instead of going to an airport we went to the harbour to get on the plane, which was waiting on the water. The plane takes off and lands on the water – it's scary but amazing! The view from the plane was beautiful because it flew so close to the water. The sea was so blue and clear and you could see all the pretty islands and the sandy beaches as you flew over them. I'll never forget it!

Unit 19 The natural world

Vocabulary

1 Across: 1 monkey 4 tiger 5 frog 6 parrot 7 donkey 9 butterfly 12 fish 13 zebra 14 mosquito 15 penguin
Down: 2 kangaroo 3 giraffe 7 dolphin 8 duck 10 elephant 11 shark 14 mouse

2 1 planet 2 sky 3 moon 4 star 5 bush 6 leaves 7 branches 8 species 9 continent 10 ice

Speaking

Suggested answers:

1 Where I live there's a lot of wildlife. There are lots of birds because I live near a big river. There are dolphins in the river too. And lots of fish.

2 My favourite season is winter because then we can go to the mountains and go hiking. In the summer it's too hot and in the spring and autumn it rains too much to go there.

3 Where I live there's a lot of farmland, so there are lots of fields and some small woods.

4 Yes, I've been to the mountains many times. It's lovely there. The air is very clean, and the sky is very blue. There are lots of lovely flowers that grow on the mountain. It's especially beautiful at sunrise.

5 Yes, I think it's very important to look after the natural world. We have to protect the animals and the land. If we don't, then our grandchildren will not be able to see all the wonderful things we have on the planet.

Reading

1 A **2** B **3** D

Grammar Box

Sample answer:

Whereas elephants are very big, fish are much smaller.

Fish swim in the sea, while elephants live on land.

Although elephants move slowly most of the time, they sometimes move fast.

Listening

1 B   2 C   3 A

Writing

Sample answer:

Jane could see that the baby elephant was hurt. Its leg was bleeding badly. She looked around but she couldn't see any other elephants. Although she knew she shouldn't touch a wild animal, Jane couldn't just leave it there to die. Carefully she walked up to it and spoke calmly. Then she took some bandages out of her backpack and tied them around the elephant's leg. Her patient watched her as she worked. Then Jane heard a noise. Oh no! It was the mother elephant. Quickly Jane packed up her bag and ran to the nearest trees just in time as the mother ran to her baby. The baby stood up and slowly followed its mother into the jungle.

Unit 20 Language

Vocabulary

1 Across: 6 translation 7 argue 8 meaning
   9 chat 10 mention
   Down: 1 communication 2 beginner
   3 vocabulary 4 intermediate 5 joke

2 1 ask 2 mean 3 email 4 pronounce 5 talk
   6 answer 7 tell 8 speak 9 translate
   10 mention

Speaking

Sample answer:

I think the photos all show really good ways to practise another language. For example, it's great to watch films or to listen to music in that language, as they're fun and you hear lots of different vocabulary and grammar. Do you agree? I think reading books is good but it's not the best way, because you need to have a good level to understand a book, or you have to use a dictionary all the time and that's annoying. I think the most interesting ways to practise a language are to talk to people who speak that language, either in groups or online, or by visiting a country where people speak it. This is probably the best way because you hear the language everywhere and you have to use it to communicate with people in shops and in hotels and other places. But, of course, it's not always possible to go to another country. I also like using language apps to practise my English. Would you agree?

Reading

1 C   2 B   3 B

Grammar Box

1 in   2 by   3 on

Listening

1 B   2 C   3 A   4 B

Grammar Box

1 of   2 for   3 with   4 to   5 on

Writing

Sample answer:

Dear Mr Thomas,

Thank you for the offer of extra English classes. I think this would be very helpful.

I think it would be best to focus on grammar and vocabulary as I think these are very important in the exam.

It would suit me to do the classes before school on either Mondays or Tuesdays. I could also do them after school on Fridays. I'd prefer not to do them at lunchtime as I do some sports clubs at lunchtimes.

I find the topics of technology and the natural world quite difficult as there is so much vocabulary to remember, so could we look at those, please?

Thanks!

Jasmine

Word Lists

Unit 1

Clothes and accessories

backpack
bracelet
cotton
dress
earring
glasses
handbag
kit
label
laundry
make-up
material
necklace
pattern
perfume
pocket
raincoat
ring
silk
size
socks
tracksuit
underwear
uniform
woollen

Unit 2

Education

art lesson
classroom
clever
college
course
degree
dictionary
exams
lessons
level
library
music lesson
notes

pencil case
primary
project
pupil
qualification
remember
research
rubber
ruler
teacher
university

Unit 3

Food and drink

barbecue
beans
broccoli
cabbage
coconut
cucumber
flour
herbs
ingredients
melon
microwave
onion
pan
peach
peanut
picnic
pie
recipe
refreshments
restaurant
salmon
slice
snack
sour
spicy
sweet
takeaway
taste
toast
vegetarian

Unit 4

Hobbies and leisure

campsite
chess
cruise
festival
gallery
go out
go shopping
guitar
hang out
hiking
ice skates
ice skating
jogging
join in
keen on
opening hours
party
playground
sculpture
sightseeing
sunbathing

Unit 5

House and home

antique
apartment
balcony
barbecue
blind
bowl
bulb
ceiling
cellar
clothes line
cottage
cupboard
drawer
entrance
flatmate
fridge
front door

furniture
garage
garden
gate
handle
ladder
light
lock
microwave
mug
neighbour
oven
path
property
rent
roof
sink

Unit 6

Personal feelings, opinions and experiences

amazing
anxious
ashamed
boring
bossy
challenging
cheerful
confusing
cruel
cute
delighted
disappointed
embarrassed
excited
frightening
generous
gentle
interested
jealous
miserable
patient
reliable
rude
unusual

Unit 7

Sport

athlete
athletics
boxing
champion
changing room
competitor
court
cyclist
extreme sport
goalkeeper
gymnastics
helmet
ice hockey
ice skating
motor-racing
pitch
race track
rider
sailing
skiing
snowboarding
stadium
water skiing
yoga

Unit 8

Work and jobs

apply
babysitter
butcher
chef
cleaner
crew
detective
full-time
guard
guest
hairdresser
journalist
judge
lecturer
librarian
novelist
nurse

part-time
retire
salary
soldier
unemployed
vet
volunteer

Unit 9

Entertainment and media

actor
audience
ballet
band
camera
circus
fireworks
guitarist
headphones
hero
interval
interviewer
journalist
musician
orchestra
performer
play (n)
podcast
presenter
record (v)
row (n)
scene
selfie
series
song
stage
studio
talk show
theatre

Unit 10

Communication and technology

app
blog

blogger
calculator
chat room
data
delete
download
email
envelope
homepage
invention
keyboard
laptop
mouse
parcel
password
photo/photograph
podcast
postcard
ring (v)
robot
text message
upload
video clip
volume
webcam

Unit 11

Health, medicine and exercise

accident
ankle
bandage
bone
brain
diet
earache
emergency
finger
foot
gym
hand
headache
heel
knee
leg
operation
painful

patient
pharmacy
pill
prescription
sick
toes

Unit 12

Places: Buildings

apartment block
bookshop
café
clinic
college
department store
entrance
exit
factory
gallery
garage
grocery store
guest-house
hotel
library
lift
office
palace
prison
ruin
stadium
tourist information centre
tower
university

Unit 13

Places: Countryside

bay
canal
cliff
desert
earth
field
forest
harbour
hill
island

lake
land
mountain
ocean
port
region
rock
scenery
seaside
stream
valley
waterfall

Unit 14

Places: Town and city

airport
bridge
bus stop
cash machine
corner
crossing
crossroads
fountain
monument
motorway
park
pavement
petrol station
playground
roundabout
route
signpost
square
subway
tunnel
turning
underground
zoo

Unit 15

Environment

bin
bottle bank
cans
cardboard
climate change

factory
glass
little
petrol
plastic
pollution
prohibited
recycle
recycling
smoke
traffic
traffic jam
volunteer (n)

Unit 16

Shopping

bargain
closed
credit card
customer
damaged
exchange
expensive
label
logo
mall
money
order
pay
price
receipt
reduced
reserve
return
second-hand

Unit 17

Weather

blow
breeze
cloud
cool
degree
dry
forecast
frozen

gale
get wet
heat
humid
ice
icy
lightning
mild
rain
shower
snowfall
storm
sunshine
temperature
thunder
thunderstorm
weather

Unit 18

Travel and transport

astronaut
backpacker
brochure
by air
by land
by rail
by road
by sea
ferry
guide book
handlebars
mirror
on board
on business
on foot
on holiday
on time
parking space
rocket
waiting room

Unit 19

The natural world

branch
bush
butterfly

continent
dolphin
donkey
duck
elephant
fish
frog
giraffe
kangaroo
leaf
monkey
moon
mosquito
mouse
parrot
penguin
planet
shark
sky
species
star
tiger
zebra

Unit 20

Language

answer
argue
ask
beginner
chat
communication
email
intermediate
joke
mean
meaning
mention
pronounce
speak
talk
tell
translate
translation
vocabulary